AFTER BOTHAM

by Allisa Charles-Findley
Jeremiah Cobra

chalice
PRESS

Print: 9780827201132
EPUB: 9780827201149
EPDF: 9780827201156

ChalicePress.com

Printed in the United States of America

Contents

Foreword

I have sat here looking at my computer screen for a quite a while, thinking on how best to introduce you to Allisa Charles-Findley and the experience you're about to read. When I consider it, I must filter through all of my own emotions of frustration, impatience, incredulity, sadness, and righteous anger to get to that place of speaking calmly once more.

Allisa Charles-Findley should not have the story she is about to tell you.

If her brother had been a white man lying on his own couch in his own apartment, she very well may not have this story. We will never know. As she says here, the only one who truly knows why the events unfolded in her brother's apartment that night is his murderer, the off-duty police officer who killed him in his own home while he lay on his own couch watching a game and eating ice cream.

But the story of Botham Jean did not end with Amber Guyger's snap decision to pull a gun and shoot. Her action and his death are not the complete story. They *are* the story that rose to the national consciousness, just like other victims whose families I've worked with. Trayvon Martin. Breonna Taylor. George Floyd. Ahmaud Arbery. Daunte Wright. So many. You have heard the stories of those killings. And yet you have not heard beyond the initial story.

When their Black skin is held to the ground, thrown in a vehicle, or pierced by a bullet, the story of that ending of a life blankets airwaves and phone screens. We respond. We march. We fight for justice. We try to move this country further along that arc that Dr. King assured us exists.

And yet what we fail as a nation to see is that when a Black person is killed by a police officer, it is but one chapter in a full library of stories. There is the full story of the person who has been killed – beyond the moment that person died. There are also the full stories of the sisters, brothers, fathers, mothers, cousins, neighbors, church members, coworkers, friends, aunties, nieces, nephews – an entire fabric of community whose threads are pulled so taught they snap and fray. Long after the television vans move away, those people have to figure out how to weave their stories into a whole again. The pattern of their lives' fabric will never be what it could have been. It cannot be when one of the invaluable threads has been ripped away mid-weave.

We should be aware enough to consider the community without them needing to lay bare their souls. It is not the left behind's responsibility to show us their hurt, to open our eyes and hearts and minds to the aftermath so that maybe we can feel the kindred humanity and care enough to pursue justice and prevention.

But, 68 years after Emmett Till's mama laid her baby boy bare so all could see the violence and its aftermath, we are still not a nation that thinks about what comes after. Not yet.

We are, as I write this, still a nation that treats a killer differently if it comes bearing a badge.

When Amber Guyger took Botham Jean's life on September 6, 2018, she murdered more than Bo. She killed his community. She silenced his rich baritone that flowed out across the congregation from the pulpit at Dallas West Church of Christ every Sunday. She ripped away his mother's ability to ever feel her boy's arms around her again. She left a gaping hole at his desk at PricewaterhouseCoopers. She robbed Harding University of a future executive as an alumnus and Saint Lucia of a rising star.

She tore away Allisa Charles-Findley's best friend. Her brother.

Each time I receive a call from another family, I see the endings that happen as a result of a police officer choosing violence. I see that aftermath, all those ripped threads, that massacre of what was becoming a beautiful image. I bear witness to it.

And now, thanks to Allisa, so will you.

May her offering here find resonance in your soul as it did mine.

*— **Ben Crump***

Chapter One

My mind was not my own.

I couldn't remember how I'd gotten in the plane. It was as if I'd always been there. Flying. High in the sky. Up among the clouds. So many clouds. I should have felt something. A certain weightlessness, perhaps. But I felt nothing. Not the wind turbulence occasionally moving the plane. Not the cabin air around me. Yet still, I knew I was flying. Like a ghost.

"Ma'am, would you like something to drink?" I heard a voice say into my ear.

No. How can I drink anything at a time like this?

"Ma'am?" I heard the voice again—a woman's voice.

I said no. Why are you still here?

"Ma'am, are you okay?" she asked.

"No." The sound of my own voice snapped me back to reality. I *was* flying. On a Boeing 747 headed to Texas. To my baby brother. Wouldn't he be so surprised to see me?

"No," I said again. "No, I am not okay."

"So you *would* like something to drink?" The young flight attendant smiled, appearing friendly enough. Her smile was the only thing I noticed about her. Certainly she had other noteworthy attributes, like hair, ears, hands, a body—all the components people were supposed to have. But I wouldn't remember any of them.

She kept talking, but I had already stopped hearing. So much of the day's occurrences had become a blur. I couldn't even remember walking through LaGuardia Airport. Couldn't remember waiting at the gate. Couldn't remember boarding the plane. The last thing I truly remembered was speaking with Botham.

"Guess where I'm heading, Big Sis?" he had asked me on our FaceTime call the previous day. My commute back home in New York City during rush hour was often a perfect time for our daily chat. I was an hour ahead of Botham, so when I took his call at 5:29 p.m., I did not expect him to also be heading home. Nevertheless, on September 6 I recall hearing the joy in my brother's voice; it was a bit more intense and contagious than usual. I could not help laughing even before he told me his good news.

"Where are you heading?" I asked, mirroring his smile.

"Home!" Botham exclaimed. "Apparently, a bit of rain in Texas means everyone gets to go home." Botham loved his job at PricewaterhouseCoopers, where he had been an accountant since graduating from Harding University two years prior. PwC is one of the Big Four accounting firms worldwide, and Botham had worked hard to secure a position there. He'd been so proud to get his degree, and I will never forget his smile when he framed his diploma.

But if graduating from Harding was Botham's proudest achievement, securing a position at PwC was his second proudest. He loved the work he did at that firm, and the firm loved him in return. Still, he was ecstatic about the prospect of ending his day early, even if it came with inclement weather. That was one of the things I loved most about Botham, how easily he could find the silver lining in a rain cloud.

"And what are you gonna do with all of this new free time?" I asked, still smiling. How could I not smile? His joy had always been so infectious.

"What do you think?" he asked. "The dentist says I'm finally free from eating soup. So I'm gonna celebrate with as much ice cream as I can carry out the store!"

"Well, just be careful," I replied. "Don't eat the whole tub in one night."

"And why not?" He chuckled. "I've earned it!"

"Too much sugar," I protested, startling myself once again to reality on the airplane. I looked around a bit sheepishly, realizing I had said those last words out loud.

"So no sugar?" a different, slightly older woman asked with the same pleasant-enough smile. I looked back at her, dumbfounded. Only then did I notice that the first flight attendant had moved several rows away. I didn't know how long this second attendant had been standing there. I looked to my mother, but her eyes had not opened.

"Sugar for your tea?" the woman repeated.

"What?" I turned back to her.

"No cream, but how about sugar?" she asked.

"No," I said. "Just tea." She placed the cup of steaming-hot liquid on the tray before me. Perhaps that tray had always been there, lowered in front of me. Just like I had always been there. Flying. I stared at the tea-filled paper cup, confused.

I don't drink plain tea.

I did not trust my hands to reach for that cup any more than I trusted my body to be on this plane. How could I be on a plane? Sure, I vaguely recalled booking the ticket to Dallas, but I would have only done that if something was wrong. I had gone to work that morning. How could I have started the day as usual if something was wrong?

You went to work because you go to work every day. Everything must be fine if you're doing what you have always done, right? Wake up. Pray. Get the boys ready for school. Get the boys ready . . . Get the boys . . .

I had spoken to my three sons just a few hours ago, explaining things to them before I left for the airport.

Last night . . . I remembered saying as I looked into the brown, expectant eyes of my eldest son Jayden, my second son Jareem, and my youngest son Jordan, who was only three years old and probably would not even remember this conversation. *I mean, this morning I got a call about your Uncle Botham. Well, I got a call last night and another one this morning. He is . . .*

"Excuse me!" an urgent voice interrupted my thoughts, and I was startled to discover that it was my own. I was walking up the aisle, past the rows of other passengers, past the older flight attendant, who now looked at me with concern. The aisle seemed incredibly long, but soon I was at the lavatory door. Relieved it was unoccupied, I pushed my way into the tiny space, locked the door, and breathed a heavy sigh. I tried to calm myself, but a wave of nausea overcame me. I looked into the small, cloudy mirror, trying hard to remember what I'd said to my three sons.

Last night, I got a call about your Uncle Botham. He is fine. Perfectly fine. I mean, he is in trouble. A little trouble. Nothing he can't handle. And he can handle anything. You see, this trouble has him in a place where we can't reach him. We won't be able to reach him for some time while he goes through . . . witness protection, I think they called it. Yeah, that's it. He's in witness protection. And we won't be able to talk to him until . . .

"No," I said to my reflection. "That's not what I told them because that's not true.

But wouldn't it be easier if . . . ?

"No."

A knock at the lavatory door interrupted my thoughts.

"Everything okay in there?" The young attendant's voice seemed only inches from the door, making the room feel even smaller. I quickly unlocked the door and pulled it open.

"I am fine," I replied, smiling as best I could. I pushed past her and headed back to my seat where my mother, Allison Jean, remained motionless, her eyes still closed. There was no furrow in her brow, no quiver in her lip. I wanted to pry her eyes open to see if she was as peaceful as she seemed, or if she was going through the same hell that I was. I sat down next to her and closed my eyes, although

I had no intention of sleeping. How could I sleep? Nevertheless, I dreamed. Perhaps that is all my mother was doing: dreaming about the way Botham must have been last night—snuggled up on his sofa, holding a big tub of vanilla ice cream.

Milky Way. That was our nickname for him because Botham loved dairy: milkshakes, eggnog, cereal with milk, and—of course—ice cream. He loved ice cream the most. He was always happy when he had some and would smile when he knew he was going to get some. I will never forget that smile of his: a little uneven on the right corner, but always wide, always joyful.

Not anymore. Last night was the last time Botham would eat ice cream and the last time he would smile. Last night, the night of September 6, 2018, a police officer entered his home and killed him.

Now, I was on my way to see my brother, who would not be surprised to see me. He wouldn't see me at all. Botham was dead. A cop had shot him. He was killed in his own home while he ate ice cream. And my mind suddenly raced to find a reason.

Thus began the biggest test I'd ever had in my life. A test of my faith, my sanity, my life. I wondered, *Is this your will, Lord? To test me for the rest of my days? I do not know if I am that strong.*

But as the plane began its descent into Dallas/Fort Worth International Airport, an emptiness hit me as I came to the sudden realization that Botham would not be there to greet me. He did not know I was in town. He would never know.

When my feet touched the ground, I would be starting a life after Botham. But I was not yet ready to turn away from my life before.

Chapter Two

Botham was born ten years after me. Our mother is Allison Jean, but we have different fathers. His father is Bertrum Jean. Maybe he got his musicality from his father. I mean, I enjoyed music, but Botham love-loved it. He was a musical baby. Before he could even crawl, he would rock and wiggle back and forth to whatever music was playing. He understood rhythm before he could talk. When he was only six years old, he would sneak off with my tapes and CDs.

Jay-Z. *Hard Knock Life.*

That one was my favorite. I always noticed when it was missing, and Botham would always become sheepish when he had to admit he'd taken it.

And boy, could my brother sing! Botham started singing in our church before he was eight years old. He also wanted to be baptized young, but at age eight was told he was too young and would have to wait until he was ten. He was allowed sing all he wanted at church though. By the time he was a teenager, he was preaching at our church, and we all knew he had found his calling. Not only could Botham sing his whole heart out; he found himself in a position to teach the choir how to read music, keep the rhythm, project their voices, and sing with their whole hearts. He would later teach the choir at his university. When I heard them perform, I knew he had shared with them a large measure of his soul. Oh, how they sang like him.

I remember the last time I watched Botham conduct his university choir. He stood before them like a ship's captain, guiding every hymn and note from their mouths with a self-assured hand. His shoulders, which looked like they could carry the weight of an entire congregation, had grown broad like a warrior's but were made regal by the tailored suit jacket he wore. Though he wasn't wearing a tie, I can't help but think that if he had worn one, it would have been his favorite color: red. And not just any red, but a passionate, vibrant shade. I was his elder sister, but looking at him in his element, I wanted to be like him. Be like Bo, as I lovingly called him.

He conducted me once, late in the summer of 2007. He was only sixteen at the time, and one of our cousins, Andrea, was getting married. Botham wanted to sing Kelly Clarkson's "A Moment Like This" at her wedding, along with Aunt Desma and me. He tried his very best to share a bit of that passion he had for music. If only we could just get the notes right.

"Yeah . . . no," he said as Aunt Desma and I joined him in laughter, shaking with hysterics. "I don't know which notes those were, but they're not the ones to this song."

My ears grew warm, and that warmth spread to the nape of my neck and all around my collar. I knew that I was the one who had not hit the right note. "Don't worry though," he encouraged. "We'll get it." I was sure my cheeks had also grown flush with embarrassment, but the feeling quickly faded as I reveled in Botham's humor and resolve. He was too young to be guiding me the way he was, yet I felt perfectly secure following his instruction.

"Catch me when I fall," Botham sang. Then he explained how to emphasize words. "You have to come up on the word *catch*." He demonstrated the note twice more before Aunt Desma and I tried again.

"That's it!" he said, delighted. "See? I knew you could get that note."

"Now we just need to get it in front of dozens of people," Aunt Desma said.

"On the most important day of Andy's life," I chimed in.

"And we'll be great," Botham reassured. "Trust me." His grin was reassuring, and for a moment I forgot about all the eyes and ears that would be on me at the wedding.

"Let's take it from the top," he said.

I filled my lungs with air and exhaled the notes, feeling their frequencies vibrate in my chest and head. I heard them mingle perfectly with Desma's soprano notes while Botham anchored us with his baritone. My confidence began to grow as we approached the chorus. My eyes were glued to Botham's steadying hand as he guided us through the troublesome high notes and the notes we had to hold the longest.

By the time we reached the end of the song, there was a divine resonance that seemed to spread from within our bodies, out through the entirety of my mother's living room, and all over the island of Saint Lucia. I felt that I could go into a recording studio and lay background vocals for Kelly Clarkson herself. But then we separated. Desma went to the kitchen as Botham, most noticeably, went to his room, closing the door with a resolute thud behind him. The hallway darkened, and I found myself alone in the living room, beginning to doubt myself.

I imagined standing before the attendants of the wedding, family, and friends. I feared I would not be able to breathe into my diaphragm the way Botham had taught me. I feared I would not be able to open my mouth wide enough or get my tongue out of the way. What if my voice got caught in my throat, making it sore? Then my voice would sputter from my lips in a croak, shattering the harmonies into an array of disjointed, dissonant chords. I would look around at the disappointed faces, but none would hurt me so much as Botham's face if I failed him. I was determined to not do that.

The day before the wedding, I tried to back out of the performance.

"You should do it yourself," I said. "You're good at this. I can't be that good."

"Did you not hear yourself yesterday?" he declared. "Did you hear us? We're amazing, and we'll be amazing at the wedding.

Together." He put his arm around my shoulders and enveloped me with his embrace. At nearly six feet, Botham was already nearly a foot taller than me. I did not know what it was like to embrace my own father in this way; he was out of the picture when I was very young. Although I had always been Big Sis to Botham, in that moment, with him towering over me, I felt protected and my confidence returned. Perhaps I really could do it after all.

"And besides," Botham continued, "can you imagine a big ol' burly dude up there singing Kelly Clarkson by myself? I'd look crazy! I need you up there with me."

When we practiced that day, the sound of our voices harmonizing made me feel giant once again.

"I think we're ready," Botham said at the end of the session, and I believed him.

The day of the wedding was perfectly tropical. The sun shone brightly on the horizon and the sky became a deep, cobalt shade of blue. The ocean breeze rustled the leaves on the gum trees, mingling with their scent and carrying them through every open window in the church. The songs of black finches and island parrots also rode that wind current. Their music was subtle outside of the window, but I heard it clearly. I soon became anxious with the prospect of singing in front of the many people who were filling the pews. I tried to keep my mind on Botham's encouraging words, but the chatter of those in attendance began to drown them out. Then I noticed the birdsong again. And the sound of my beating heart. These sounds swelled and swirled around me. Even my tongue felt as though it would block my throat and keep me from breathing. When Botham approached me, he must have seen a truly pitiful creature because his expression instantly became sympathetic.

"I can't," I blurted out when it seemed Botham was close enough to hear me over the noise.

"I'm right here," he said. "You don't have to shout."

"I can't," I said, softly this time.

"You can't what?" he asked.

"I can't sing."

"Of course you can! You sing beautifully. You've *been singing* beautifully all weekend."

It wasn't that I did not believe Botham. Together, I knew we would sound great. But he had arranged the song so that we each sang our verses solo. It would just be me for the second verse. Me, alone.

"I mean, I can't sing in front of everyone," I said. "Not by myself."

"You can," he assured me. "You're just nervous, and that's okay. Everyone gets nervous. I would even say you're supposed to be nervous. I could tell you how to overcome it. Perhaps you can picture everyone naked, but that's not necessary. You just have to sing. Also, picturing our entire family naked . . . Well, that would be gross."

I forced a smile. He was not convinced that his humor had overcome my anxiety.

"You will be great," he assured. By this time, Desma had approached us both.

"What's wrong?" she asked.

"I'm not going to sing," I said resolutely, knowing that if I let him, Botham would talk me into it. And I had already surrendered my nerve. I would not find my voice on that day.

"Well, if she's not gonna do it, I'm not either," Desma said. Although Desma was my aunt, she was only two years older than I and felt more like a cousin to me. On the day of the wedding, we wore our hair in a similar updo, and our dresses had similar shades of yellow and brown. We stood together in our refusal to sing, so we outnumbered Botham. I saw the disappointment settle into his whole body. He all but pouted, and I was again aware that he was hardly old enough to drive. I wanted to hug him until I remembered that I was the reason for his being upset.

"Fine," he said quietly. "I can't make you." Then he walked away, dejected. I felt both awful and relieved. Botham had a love of singing, but I didn't, yet I knew how excited he had been to bestow his gift of song to our cousin. It was the only gift he could afford that was worthy of his admiration for her, and I had denied him the chance to give it.

Next time, I thought. *I won't refuse him next time. Next time, whatever the circumstances, I'll find my voice for him.*

The wedding was beautiful. Andrea was stunning in her gown. She and her beau said "I do" under the orange sun and cobalt sky. Then we were off to the reception where we ate, drank, and danced until the sunset sky turned pink and purple. At some point during the reception, I thought to find Botham and see how he was doing. As our time to sing came and went without a single note from Desma, Botham, or me, my guilt at having refused his wish grew and grew. I also knew that his anger was a quiet one, much more akin to sadness, and it worried me that at such a festive time, he might be in some corner brooding. However, just as I stood to go find Botham, I saw him emerge from the crowd on the dance floor. With a smile as wide as it ever was, he sauntered over to me as if he had the most fantastic secret to share with me.

"Dancing is not for everyone," he said quietly when he was close enough that only I would hear him.

"I don't know whose side of the family this guy is on," Botham said between fits of laughter, "but it isn't the side with rhythm." Of course his laughter was contagious, so I joined in without even knowing who he was talking about.

"Just out of curiosity, what kind of dance move is this?" he asked, imitating what he had seen someone doing just moments earlier. Perhaps the dance was supposed to be the Bogle except that Botham was moving in feigned, exaggerated spasms to the song by Tony Matterhorn blaring through the speakers. He transitioned to some form of the Butterfly and said, "Look, the wings are broken!" Then he placed his hands on his knees and began whipping his head back and forth.

"Dutty Wine!" he cried before tilting his head back and hollering with laughter.

"I don't know what any of those are, but you should make him stop," I said. "That's not dancing. That's a medical condition!"

"Ha!" Botham said. "I'll go get him some help then."

He disappeared into the crowd again, and with him went all of the guilt and anxiety I had been feeling over the past few days.

Botham's anger was never loud, and it never lingered. As the reception came to an end, I even wondered if he had not put on that little performance just for me. Just as I had wondered if he was still upset about not singing, he always seemed to know when I was feeling upset about something. The only difference is that he seemed to know exactly what to do to alleviate the tension. The night of Andreas's wedding, he knew exactly what to do to put me in a good mood, even when I was the one who had caused the tension between us. It might be easy to assume that Botham simply had a short memory and a strong desire to dance out of rhythm. But his timing had been too perfect. Whatever the case might have been, I will remember that wedding for the way he lifted me up twice: once when I did not even know how high I could soar, and again when my own disbelief in myself brought me low.

* * *

As my mother and I rode in the taxi from the Dallas airport to our hotel, I pictured Botham's smile. Then the idea that I would never see it again occurred to me. I wanted more than anything to turn back time. I prayed and asked God to turn back time. Of course, He did not.

I knew then that all of this must have been His will. This was a test for me to see what I could endure. God wanted to see if I could be like Job, if I could still live by His will and follow His Word after he took away one of the biggest blessings I had in this world. It is said that He gives only the biggest tests to His strongest children. So He was testing my faith. But why should my test cost me so much? And why had Botham been the one to pay the ultimate price?

Perhaps his life was the cost for a greater cause, a greater good. After all, wasn't Botham the perfect victim? Before him, others had always manufactured some excuse for why White police officers were killing Black people: "That Black man was resisting arrest!" "Maybe it was the drugs in his system, not the knee on his neck, that stopped him from breathing." "Maybe he reached too quickly for his wallet." Or "That Black woman was in the wrong place around the wrong people." But there was nothing for them to twist here, nothing to spin, no lie to conjure against Botham. Botham was a church pastor and a college-graduate professional who'd been in the *right* place doing the *right* thing around the *right* people—in his own home by himself minding his business. How could the police twist that? He was in the right place at the wrong time?

Was this just one more innocent life, or would it be that last one, the one that would shine a light on and put an end to police brutality? And if so, must that be my cost? Because no one else has to pay it, only me and the rest of his family.

Botham was only a beautiful, innocent man to us.

Yet he was a scary silhouette to the cop who shot him.

A statistic to politicians and lawmakers.

He was just another name and a few pictures to the media and those who will only ever know him through the media.

They never told the joke that made him smile. They never heard him sing. They never watched him direct a choir. They did not know how he suffered from a recent dental surgery and was overjoyed to finally eat ice cream on the night—last night—when he was killed. They did not see the horror on his face as he looked down the barrel of that gun and wondered what was happening or what he had possibly done wrong. They did not know him in his real life. And they will not suffer in their real lives. Not like I had suffered in the twenty-four hours since I'd heard about his death.

Not like I will suffer for the rest of my days.

Chapter Three

9:00 a.m.

That was the time I was told to expect the call from the Baylor Police Department about Botham on the morning after his shooting.

It was 12:29 a.m. when I received the call from Baylor University Medical Center, informing me that my brother had been shot. He'd been alone in his apartment when a police officer entered through his front door, aimed her gun at him, and shot him. Center mass.

It was 12:45 a.m. when I hung up. At first, I did not believe what I had heard. Surely this call was a mistake.

I stared at the clock on my bedside table for what seemed like hours before it changed to read 12:46 a.m. Several minutes passed as I resisted the urge to call Botham. Who else would I call with such awful news? He had been my person, the one I would call with any news—good, bad, significant, or mundane. And here was the worst, most significant news I had ever received in my life. I wanted to call my person.

In shock, I picked up my phone and called my mother. She was already crying when she answered.

"They killed my son," she said once, twice, and then a third time. Each time was followed by wailing that would wane over several minutes into a sob before she repeated the words that tore at my heart each time I heard them. I did not expect such surrender from her. My mother always presented herself as a woman of intellect and education, a woman of distinction. She was college educated, and she had held prominent positions in Saint Lucia's government. I didn't know how a mother ought to respond when she first hears that she has lost her son. But I did not expect surrender.

I listened in stony silence until the third time. "They said they would call me in the morning." I hoped the utterance of future expectations would soften the harsh moment. As my mother continued sobbing, I searched for other things to say.

"I have to get the boys off to school in the morning," I said absentmindedly. "And maybe I'll get to work a little late." But my mother did not seem to hear me. She only continued sobbing. That's when I began to feel the anger rise in me. Not for her sadness or her tears. Not because she was repeatedly giving utterance to something I refused to accept. I was angry because she had been willing to accept something I refused to accept.

Botham wasn't dead. He couldn't be. Tomorrow, I would wake up at 6:30 a.m. and pray for my family the way I always did. I would pray for my mother and father. I would pray for my sons. And I would pray for Botham, for his health and happiness. Then I would get my boys ready for school. The two oldest might get into a boasting match over who could beat Uncle Botham when they saw him next. Or maybe they would express their excitement over the first Giants game of the season. And I would have a little time in the kitchen with my youngest—and a cup of coffee—before his older brothers came down for breakfast.

After I dropped them off, I would get to work early as I usually did. I would check a few emails before I headed out for a few appointments. If all went well, perhaps I would be done before lunch. Plenty of time to read the news and find something ridiculous or humorous to send to Botham. That would make his day. Then we could talk about it during rush hour, my favorite time of the day because of our check-ins. If he called first, I would know it was him even before I looked at my phone. Yesterday, we laughed about the man who burned his house down trying to set fire to a pair of Nikes because they ran a campaign with Colin Kaepernick. Today, I would find something funnier or thought-provoking. He would like that.

So why was my mother saying this about him? How could she so easily accept Botham's death as fact? Maybe it was all a mistake. And if it wasn't, she should pretend. It hadn't even been an hour since we'd gotten the phone call, and already she was saying goodbye. Goodbye to her son.

I hung up with my mother and called Aunt Desma, but she was as upset as my mother. I could not bear their tears. I wanted someone to tell me that this had all been some kind of mistake. I wanted to hold on to some hope that the phone call I would get in the morning would confirm their mistake: it wasn't really Botham who was killed but someone who looked like him. So I got off the phone with my aunt as quickly as I could and stared at the clock.

* * *

1:09 a.m.

My imagination began to run wild. I could not help picturing Botham sitting in his living room, the bullet going straight through the front door, shattering the magnetic lock on the way in, and piercing his heart. Then I pictured it going through a tub of ice cream before it reached him. The ice cream ought to have stopped the bullet. Or the Bible should have. I remembered hearing a story about a man who was saved by a Bible he kept in his breast pocket. The bullet stuck in that Bible, and the man lived.

Lord, why couldn't You have given him a Bible in that moment? Or a hymn book? Where was Your divine justice tonight?

* * *

2:31 a.m.

Botham and I had recently discussed his upcoming September 29 birthday. Perhaps I could have gotten him to fly up here to New York for that weekend. His nephews would have loved that. *Maybe Jayden can finally beat him in basketball now. Maybe Botham can finally beat Jareem in Super Mario Brothers.*

We should've been picking out your cake. Now we will have to pick out your casket.

* * *

3:16 a.m.

I tried to push from my mind the fact that I had just given someone permission to take Botham's organs. That is one of the first conversations you have with a stranger when you're still trying to process the sudden end of a life.

I was trying to hold on to a world in which my heart was still whole, and it seemed no one would let me.

"Botham was an organ donor," the voice had said on the other end of the phone not long after midnight. "We do not have much time to secure them. Do we have your permission to proceed?"

"Proceed?" I asked.

"We can save many lives," said the voice.

Save his life! I wanted to shout.

"Ma'am?"

"What will you take?" I asked shakily.

"Well, ma'am . . ." The voice paused and cleared his throat before continuing. "For tissues, we would take the eyes, skin, and bone. For organs, we remove the kidneys, lungs, liver . . ."

Heart. Leave his heart. If you take it, you'll take mine with it.

"Ma'am?"

"Yes?"

"We need the family's permission for Botham Jean to donate his organs. Do you give your permission?"

"Yes."

* * *

4:44 a.m.

He didn't say "I love you" before we ended our call yesterday. He usually did. We had our usual banter though. I let him know that the Dallas Cowboys were going to be trash this season. He said the same about the Giants. We both talked trash about the Eagles, who were playing that night.

"Bah-bye," we nearly said in unison. It was only a few minutes after the call ended that I realized what he'd forgotten to say.

I'll give him hell for that next time we speak.

* * *

6:29 a.m.

My eyes were heavy from the weight of the night and dry from the tears I did not shed. I hesitated to climb out of bed, wondering for the first time in my life whether I should even bother with prayer. I would never pretend to be perfect, but I always tried to do everything I was taught to do by our church. And the Church of Christ is a strict religion in which women have little to no voice. Still, I kept my head down. I softened my voice to the point of losing it at times. And I prayed. But what would I pray for now? What good would it do? I had prayed last night for my brother's safety, only to be awakened a few short hours later with the news that God had forsaken that prayer.

When I thought about waking my boys, my very next idea was to fabricate an alternate reality regarding Botham. I could call a family meeting, talk to my mother and father, talk to my aunt, talk to my sons, and tell them that this was the way forward.

Botham was not dead. He had witnessed something awful, but it had not killed him. It could not have. It had happened to his neighbor. Botham had been walking up the stairs with a tub of ice cream tucked under his arm when he heard a scream. He'd gone toward the disturbance, and that is when he'd seen the crime. And the culprit. He'd seen the murderer, and she had seen him. No, it was a he—a big, overbearing man. But the murderer fled, and now Botham had to hide in a witness protection program. That is what happened.

And perhaps that sounded implausible, but not any crazier than the reality—that a police officer would enter an innocent man's home and shoot him for no reason. The former sounds far more likely. Anyway, it would be easier to pretend the falsehood than to deal with what really happened to Botham.

* * *

Seventy-two hours.

That's how long a killer gets to straighten out their story if that killer is a police officer. Twenty-four of those hours were gone by the time my mother and I arrived at the Omni Hotel for check-in. When we arrived at the police station the next morning, more than enough time had passed for Botham's killer to forget a few things.

The police station was a five-minute drive from the South Side Flats where Botham lived—and died. It was a rigid building of glass and brick, new and modern. It looked like a prison.

My mother and I sat on the hard wooden benches, surrounded by men and women with guns, waiting to be seen by Chief of Police Renee Hall. I felt like I was in hostile territory. The people here were not purposed with serving and protecting me. Not at all. They meant to evade my questions, to deny my attempts to learn what had happened to my brother. This much was clear once we finally had a chance to meet with Hall.

"After seventy-two hours," she explained. "That is when she has to provide her account of what happened that night."

"*Last* night," I said. "It happened last night, and the killer has not been arrested yet? Is she on the run?"

"I am sorry," Hall replied.

"Is she here?" I asked.

"She is not," Hall said with a sigh and a glance at her smartwatch. "Look, I just wanted to express my condolences. I am sorry for your loss. I can only imagine what you and your mother must be going through right now."

"Can you?" I snapped. "Can you imagine it? Because if you could, you would understand why I want answers to my questions."

"Of course, it is perfectly reasonable to want answers—" she began.

"Then why won't you answer them?" I interrupted. "Can I at least know the name of the woman who murdered my brother?"

"I am not at liberty to say," she replied softly.

"Then what are you at liberty to say?" I asked. "If you can't tell me who did it, then can you tell me why?"

"Why?" she repeated.

"Why was he killed?"

"I do not know that."

"Was he doing something wrong?" I asked.

"I can't believe that!" my mother interjected. "He was always so careful of the company he kept, of his actions, of the places he found himself."

"And he found himself at his home," I continued. "He even thought to go out last night. We talked about how that might not be the safest thing. He was in his home. *His* home!"

"I know, Miss Findley," the chief said. "And I know this must be frustrating for you. But this is a sensitive case, and we have to be judicious about information until all the facts come out."

"The facts?" I fumed. "But you have facts. Someone in here can tell me something, I'm certain of that. Was it not your officers who responded to the call? Was it not your officer who shot..." I trailed off, searching her eyes for some semblance of humanity. Hall was a human being like me. She couldn't be impervious to pain. She had to understand the helplessness you feel when death claims someone you dearly love. How could this officer look at another human and not see the pain in her eyes. Or worse, how could she see it and look at me with such emptiness.

"I promise you"—Hall looked at her watch again—"as soon as we know more, you will too."

"But you do know something," my mother said while I stared into eyes whose color I could not see for the void staring back at me. "You have to know something." My mother began sobbing. "One of your own people killed my son. She must have walked by you this very morning!"

"I wish I could be of more help," Hall said, "but I have to prepare for a press conference. I'm told you will be at the Dallas West Church of Christ later in the afternoon. Is that correct?"

"Yes," I replied.

"The mayor and I will come by," she said, standing to take her leave. "The Texas Ranger, David Armstrong, will be there too. He may have some information as well. But he is in the same position as I."

My mother continued to fret and plead for information, but I knew none was coming. Gently, I took her by her shoulders and guided her out of the building.

"Can we at least go see his apartment?" my mother asked the detective before we reached the door.

Hall sighed. "It's a crime scene."

"We need to prepare for his funeral," my mother added. "We need his passport."

"I'll see if I can get you an escort," Hall replied.

* * *

It was a short drive to South Side Flats, not enough time to prepare for the emptiness I would find there.

We were not allowed inside, but there were plenty of things to see in Botham's apartment. The fact that I could only look from the doorway further kept me from accepting the reality of what had happened to my brother. There was something eerie about the emptiness, as if I were looking into an abyss whose bottom I could not see, or floating in the vacuum of space where nothing could be felt or heard. For the first time, I was truly beginning to grasp the idea of nothing.

No thing.

No laughter.

No singing.

No Botham.

The emptiness on the other side of that door threatened to swallow me whole. And not looking away required great effort.

Just inside the doorway, past the kitchen area but before the living room began, Botham's flip-flops lay on the faux-wood laminate floor. His desk chair sat on one side of the room, with a few of his collared shirts strewn upon it and a pair of cleats beneath it. A long, black leather sofa sat against the same wall. Against the opposite wall were a pair of his basketball shoes in front of a TV stand and flat-screen television. In the middle of the living room was an area rug and a large, brown ottoman that he must have been using as a desk because on it lay his computer, his video game controller, and the bowl of melted ice cream.

I looked with tear-blurred vision at the college diploma that sat on the far table. There was no frame for that piece of paper, yet it stood as tall and sturdy as a monument. I fixed my gaze upon that monument and marveled at its imperviousness. Then my gaze fell to the puddle of dried blood and the red footprints that covered the floor. I looked long enough to know that it was blood but looked away before I could start imagining the bodies in the shoes that tracked it all over the floor.

There were so many things in that apartment. So many things that made the room feel so very empty. The police officer entered and retrieved the suit that we would bury Botham in. The officer also found the passport we would need to have Botham's funeral in Saint Lucia. When he placed these things in my mother's arms, I could almost see the emptiness that reached out of those sleeves and grab hold of her. Her wailing echoed down the hallway. I had to take the items from her and provide consolation. When I took the suit in my hand, every memory I had of Botham spilled out in the form of his scent, and I hugged the garments tight to my chest as if doing so would keep his memory preserved.

By the time my mother and I returned to the Omni Hotel, we knew nothing more than before we had gotten on the plane. Yet I knew that had my brother been killed by a civilian and the police had caught the suspect, they would have been far more forthcoming. They would have been there to help me. Instead, I felt like a sheep who had wandered all the way from the farm just to walk into a wolves' den and ask the wolves if one of them had eaten my kinfolk.

For the next two days and nights, I watched the television and waited for the police to name my brother's killer. Instead, I saw them attempt to assassinate Botham's character—as if he were not already dead enough.

They manufactured speculations about him being a drug addict. They searched for ways in which my brother might have invited his own killing. Perhaps, they suggested, he had been waiting for someone to come into his home. Perhaps he'd been dating the killer and brought the crime of passion into his home. Maybe he was just another Black man who had neither seen nor heeded the message in the movie *Get Out*. The news speculated about all these things or referred to them as investigative findings. As if the killer could not simply be asked. As if she was nowhere to be found.

An investigator for the investigators. Who better to thwart an investigation than people who conduct them for a living? Police officers have a major advantage over criminals because most criminals are only trying to get away for the first time. But when the criminals are the police . . .

I did not feel strongly that there would be justice for Botham. His killer somehow seemed to be getting too much "right" on her side. If it were not for a civilian uploading a video of her on social media, Amber Guyger may have gotten the full seventy-two hours to be anonymous. Instead, her face was in the news by the forty-eighth hour. By the seventy-second hour, she'd been arrested. Thank God for smartphones. And while Amber Guyger was finally being taken from the comfort of her home, my family and I headed to the airport with a suit and a passport.

Chapter Four

Bo hated cemeteries. He was afraid of them. They are a place where restless souls dwell. And yet, I had returned to our birthplace to leave him in one.

I did not realize how much I missed Saint Lucia until I was back there. From the moment I exited the airport, it seemed that the breeze, at once solitary and magnificent, carried the scent of home all over Castries, Saint Lucia's capital city. I could be carried away on this breeze until I found myself in the town center, where the morning's catch lingered in the fish markets. Aromas of fresh fruit emanated from the farmers market and danced about in the air—coconuts, golden apples, cherries, plums, and other stone fruits. I could trace any one of these smells to the specific backyard where its orchards grew. So many people I knew had these fruit trees in their backyards, along with an abundance of jasmine flowers and ginger lilies. Growing up, I took for granted the sweetness those trees and blossoms lent to the air. Whenever I came home to Saint Lucia, I anticipated being reawakened to the nostalgia it triggered. But even these smells sunk like stones into the pit of my stomach when I remembered why I had returned in the first place.

This was not a trip for indulging the memories of my childhood. Not a trip for remembering how I would take Botham around in our families' backyards and indulge the delights there. Our youngest brother, Brandt, had not been born yet, so for most of Botham's childhood, it was just him and me.

Often, I would take him to Aunt Desma's house, which had mango trees in the backyard. There, Botham and I would always marvel at the green and red mounds that sprouted among the leaves at the dawn of summer. We would lay on the grass and look up at each iridescent mound holding within it a promise of euphoria. Picking the fruit had its own special magic; each branch and stem would hold firmly to the heavy fruit at first. Then, with a light snap, we would be holding that magic in our hands, a knowing that just beneath the skin was the golden flesh that would yield an almost impossible sweetness. What a grand taste of summer the mango is!

Later, Botham and I might head into our aunt's kitchen where chicken simmered with cloves of garlic and bell peppers, and homemade rotis turned golden brown in frying pans brushed with sunflower oil. If Botham had his way, there might be dasheen, breadfruit, green figs, and saltfish simmering. Once our bellies were full, a rain would fall, as it often did in summer, signaling a time for rest. No soul in Castries could resist a rainfall. No matter how busy or playful we might be, we would come inside to listen to the rain pitter-patter through the tree canopies, rustle into the green grasses, and beat against the warm, brown earth.

Botham and I would often take our naps to the staccato melody the rain played against the clay roof of our house. Botham had always been a musical child. Perhaps that rhythm was one of the reasons: the melody of rainfall, the drumming of coconuts falling in neighboring yards, the rumbling bass from the ocean waves nearby.

Depending on the time of day, any number of animals would join in the song. The whistle of the mockingbird could be heard throughout the day. Dogs barked in early evening. Roosters crowed in early morning. The trees whispered all day from the constant breeze. I always tried to discern their secrets.

But that is not why I came back to Saint Lucia this time.

Such childhood memories only haunt me now. Like ghosts in the cemeteries Botham despised. It was going to be hell for me to leave him in one.

On the day of his funeral, September 24, 2018, I sat in the church pews of Minor Basilica of the Immaculate Conception and had a hard time focusing on the words. This church—in which I had spent so many Sundays in my youth, worshiping and singing songs both joyful and somber, and which I had once considered a place of spiritual rejuvenation—now seemed like a coffin. Neither the voice of the pastor nor the song of the congregants could console me. The sermon, the hymns, and even the condolences could have very well been snarls and hisses. Those voices and the breaths that carried them from every mouth only served to make Botham's death more real. They filled the church until its air felt thick and stale in comparison to the sweet and salty air of Castries, and I could not wait to get outside. Yet when we were finally outside, the breeze had become still and every delight had dissipated in the wake of the pallbearers who, carrying Botham's casket to the hearse and then from it, cut an unswerving path to the gravesite.

When they lowered his casket into the ground, the depths of despair from which my tears and cries and howls came were unfathomable, as if I was not the one making those sounds pouring forth from my mouth. It didn't feel like my voice. Nor did it feel like my body that the pallbearers were restraining, pulling away from the open hole in the ground that held my whole world inside. They had to drag me away, but I never felt their hands or their strength. I only felt a moment that you only feel in dreams—when you are striving desperately toward a destination, but your feet never seem to carry you there.

When I returned to New York from Saint Lucia a few days later, it seemed that my soul no longer responded to my body, leaving it to go about its usual activities while my soul grieved. If I'd had to will my own heart to beat, I may not have survived. Even breathing seemed like an arduous task for my spirit. I often forgot to eat. And most days, I felt trapped inside a nightmare that would never end.

I would walk outside on unseasonably warm day, yet my body would shiver all over. Had fish begun to fly and birds to swim, I do not think I would have batted an eye.

I continued to attend church, being present in His house though my ears heard not what the preacher said, and my tongue fathomed not what it sang. When I was there, the only thought that occurred to me over and over was that Bo loved to sing. When my mind could no longer bear the memory of the thunderous baritone with which he rejoiced, my body would collapse into fits of sobs and tears. There was no consoling me in these moments, not even in His house. And in my own house, I could barely be present.

Once, when I went into my kitchen to make myself a cup of coffee, I added the half-and-half and saw very well with my own eyes the lumps that poured from the carton. With a spoon, I mushed the lumps until they dissolved like sugar cubes into the brown liquid. I hadn't meant to hurt myself. It was only that I could not interpret the threat. The food poisoning that came as a result would leave me bedridden for several days—the only days I missed from work immediately following Bo's funeral—and they passed for me the same as those days when I was not poisoned. I was lucid, but I was not awake.

One day, I found myself being held captive by this sort of lucid dreaming state in which I had allowed myself to live. That morning, I went about my routine, business as usual, except my routine had already begun to change even if I was not immediately aware of it.

First, I said a prayer filled with questions and doubts. Next, I made a cup of coffee, being sure to triple-check the cream's expiration date. Then I made a trip to the office, followed by a visit in the field. As a marketing representative, I had not only grown accustomed to visiting clients at home, I had come to excel at it. I reveled in the time away from the office, and I usually enjoyed the free time I could earn for the rest of the day if my visits were successful. I should have welcomed the chance to get away from my thoughts completely; there was no peace in my home or church, but there should have been peace at work. However, on that morning I had to visit an apartment complex. One much like the building Bo used to live in.

As I approached the building, it did not occur to me that the visit was going to go differently than any other. It was only once I parked in front of the complex that things began to feel strange. While my body had done many things without my mind having to tell it to—drinking the coffee, singing the hymns, kneeling before prayer, and driving me to where I needed to be—this time, once

I put the car in park and turned the ignition off, my body simply stopped and waited as if for a command.

At first, I was startled by its lack of motion. It seemed I was not fully prepared to do more than breathe. I looked down and noticed my body for the first time. The sleeves of my coat were no longer snug but billowed a bit around my wrists. I unfolded the visor mirror and saw that my coat and shirt collar also billowed around my neck. I realized I had not consumed much more than coffee over the past few days. When I folded the mirror up again, the apartment complex loomed in front of me, taller than before, the sun behind the clouds casting a shadow over everything.

Eager to complete my visit and get home early, I turned to the door handle. But my hand would not reach for it. I looked down at my body, which now seemed even more drowned under my layers of clothing.

I turned my gaze to the building, which was now taller and darker. I looked at the door handle again, but I could not reach for it.

Move. I thought I said the word aloud, but no sound came out of my mouth. My lips did not part. And then my breath seized in my chest. I tried to remain calm, thinking that with calm, my mind could soon command my body. But my legs did not move, nor did my hands. Before long, my car began to feel like a coffin.

I imagined Bo back in Saint Lucia.

I left him there. In the cemetery. Knowing how much he hated them.

Then I pictured him in his apartment again. He had been in the safest place he could have possibly been. And he'd died there, without even knowing why, without knowing if he had done something wrong—or if there was anything he could have done better to save his life. What is worse is that I will never be able to ask him what happened. No one will know his side of the story but him—and the cop who shot him.

Move! I shouted. But still I heard no sound. I strained with my whole heart to open the door, to get out of the car, and to walk toward that building, but my mind could not will it. All I could do was look at the apartment building and then down at my phone. I called my office, and it was only when someone answered that I found my voice again.

"I need someone to meet my nine thirty client for me," I blurted out.

"Where are you?" my colleague asked. "Are you okay?"

"I'm fine," I replied. "I'm here. But I can't get out of the car."

"Is something wrong? What do you mean you can't get out of the car?"

"I can't get out of the car!" I shouted.

"Was there an accident, or—"

"I can't get out of the car!" I cried.

"Okay, okay. Someone will be right there."

When I ended the call, my words left me again. I couldn't open the door, but I couldn't turn on the car and leave either. So I stayed and stared at the apartment complex.

And I screamed.

Chapter Five

"Hope I got some brothers that outlive me." Botham sang along with the lyrics of a new song that played on the car radio. He sat in the passenger seat as I drove him to the airport. The holiday season was over. We were only a few weeks into 2018, and it was time for Botham to return to Texas.

"Have you not seen the video to this?" he asked.

"Not yet," I replied.

"Well, you should see it, sis."

"Drake?"

"He don't miss!" Botham's voice rose with excitement. "He's so consistent. Who else has been this good for this long?"

"Jay-Z," I replied quickly. He hesitated just long enough for me to feel I had won the argument. I could feel the smirk at the corners of my lips. It didn't last.

"Not this good," he snapped.

I thought for a second and my smirk returned. "No," I replied. "Better."

"Better?" Botham was incredulous. "You need to see the video for this."

"Like what?"

"Drake just went to a random neighborhood and started giving away money," Botham explained. "One hundred seventy-five thousand dollars! Directly to the residents of Miami. Right to the people."

"No," I replied warily, "Jay-Z never did anything like that."

"See?" Botham said. I glanced at him briefly. He wore such a thoughtful expression. A hopeful one. He seemed to be looking into the future at a dream. I did not mean to tear him away from it. But still . . .

"Yeah," I began, "All Jay-Z did was bring water to several villages in Africa. Not the same." We looked at each other and burst into laughter.

"Okay, okay," Botham conceded. "You got that one. This is still a good song though."

"God's Plan."

"I want to have that kind of impact on people," Botham said.

"With music?" I asked.

"With wealth," he replied. "Well, with music too. But mostly with wealth. Imagine what we could do back home. Schools could be better. Health care . . ."

As he trailed off, I filled the silence. "All you have to do is make a platinum record," I said.

"I don't have to do that," Botham said, chuckling. "I'm doing what I ought to be doing right now. There are lots of ways to bring water to the village."

"Definitely," I said.

"Education. Organizations. We can start nonprofits."

"Sure," I said.

Then he flashed a mischievous grin and said, "But a platinum record wouldn't hurt either."

In that moment, I thought I should get Botham a ticket to a Drake concert. Drake was his favorite artist and definitely one of the inspirations in his own music. Botham directed choirs the way

Quincy Jones conducted bands. He used his voice like an instrument, layering them in multi-track a cappella recordings. He once sent me a song that sounded like a full quartet. He was becoming a self-taught song producer. Perhaps Bo was destined to have a music career in his future. Maybe his talents were supposed to grow until his music was on records.

Or maybe that wasn't God's plan.

After Botham's death, the first time I heard Drake on the radio, I reached frantically for the display on the dashboard, nearly forgetting to keep my eyes on the road. I had to listen to anything other than the words playing through my car speakers because listening to Botham's favorite artist was agony. My fingers tapped the button and found some gospel music. Still distracted, I looked up just in time to see the red brake lights of the car in front of me. I slammed on the brakes, and my purse flew from the passenger seat onto the floor, lodging itself far beneath the dashboard.

"Shit."

I was doing a lot of that lately, skipping songs that came on the radio. Sometimes the songs seemed to be speaking directly to me. Other times, they simply reminded me of Botham. Either way, I couldn't listen to them. That Drake song almost seemed like he was mocking me. But gospel wasn't any better. I needed to turn off the radio and find some music from my phone—the one in my purse.

"Shit!"

I was doing a lot of that too. Cursing, I mean. There was something satisfying about it in the same way crossing your arms in uncomfortable situations is just you giving yourself a hug.

I turned off the radio. The silence that followed was so loud. As the traffic slowed to a crawl, I longed for something to occupy my mind. When traffic stopped completely, I reached for my bag on the floor, straining my fingers until the middle one caught the strap. With the bag securely on the passenger seat, I rummaged inside until my fingers closed around my phone. I pulled it out and held it before my face. I did not like the person who stared back out of the blackness of the phone. Her face had become gaunt, and the bags were heavy under her eyes. I quickly pressed the home button, relieved by the familiar distraction.

Swipe up. Swipe left until I see my music app in the top left corner. Beside that is my phone app. Open it. Scroll to favorites.

Several weeks after his funeral, Botham's name was still at the top.

Touch his name. Botham Jean. Calling.

I let it ring once. Twice. A third time. Just as it went to voice mail, I hung up.

I'll text him later.

I was alone again in the silence. As the traffic began to move more steadily, my thoughts wandered. I was no longer behind the wheel of my Nissan; instead, I was in the cockpit of *her* SUV. The phone in my hand was no longer mine. This phone had sexually explicit messages on the screen, some sent and some received. When I placed the phone down and looked through the windshield, it was nighttime, and I was making a right turn into a parking structure I recognized. I had been here before.

Another message arrived, and I looked down just long enough to see that it was another explicit one. But I didn't reply.

This time when I looked away from the phone, I was no longer in the truck. I was walking toward the hall lined with apartment doors. Past the banisters. I stopped at a door with a red rug. Somehow, I knew I was at the right place.

This is his favorite shade.

I opened the door to a familiar face. The blue light of the television flashed on the brown skin of that face. I took a step closer, and the face looked at me. I saw the reflection of Rachel and Ross in the eyes. I knew these eyes well.

"Take me instead," she whispered. I took out a flashlight and shined it onto that brown skin and into those dark eyes, drowning out the reflection from the television.

"Leave him," she pleaded. "Take me!"

I looked at the flashlight and realized that it was fixed atop a handgun.

"Okay," I replied, my voice the same as hers.

"Thank you," she said. And I pulled the trigger.

The deafening sound of a car horn jolted me back to the Nissan. I looked around and realized that I had stopped my car in the middle of an intersection. I was now surrounded by angry faces. One man with a bushy mustache was out of his car and walking toward me.

"Are you okay?" he shouted, a bit hesitant to get too far from his car or too close to mine. "You're gonna get yourself killed sitting there. Get out of the road!"

I came to my senses and drove through the intersection, quickly pulling into a small parking lot. As I looked around, I began to recognize my surroundings. Somehow, I had made my way to Coney Island, quite far from my house in Queens. I was, however, not alarmed. I could not shake the daydream I had just had. That I had driven for nearly half an hour in the opposite direction was of very little consequence. In fact, it occurred to me that the man with the moustache was partly right. I would have gotten myself killed. And perhaps some small part of me wanted to suffer that.

If it would bring Bo back, then yes. If You would allow it. Would You?

Then, as if God had answered in the affirmative, I drove, not with the purpose of causing an accident but not with the intention of preventing one either. On the ride home that day, I remained more conscientious of the road ahead, but I made no effort to stop at red lights or mind the speed limit. My right hand, which was usually quick to the horn in the case of errant drivers around me, remained steadfast at the two o'clock position on my steering wheel. I made left turns when it suited me and dared oncoming traffic to beat me through the intersection. In truth, I was curious to see if God would answer my prayer.

And while I made my way home from Coney Island, I allowed my mind to fill the silence with its chaotic noise. So much noise. My mind drifted to the Texas Ranger who was investigating the killing.

David Armstrong was a tall, rust-colored man with wide shoulders. He had sleepy eyes, a recessed hairline, and a clean-shaven face that revealed a round, almost pudgy jawline. His expression was always stern; even when he smiled, his brow remained wrinkled with worry. Perhaps he was a decent man in his private life. Perhaps he smiled often around friends and family, told them funny jokes, and gave them warm advice. But he only showed me a cold, blank stare and a face hardened by his desire to tell me nothing about what happened to my brother. Although he was purposed with resolving Botham's murder, he was adamant about telling us nothing about Botham's murderer.

"I'm not at liberty to discuss that," he said when we asked about Amber Guyger.

"What about the other police officers who showed up?" we inquired.

"I'm not at liberty to discuss that."

"Then what can you discuss?" I asked.

"Any other questions you may have."

"Those are the only questions we have!"

Although he began our meeting by expressing his condolences and speaking of the obligation, he felt to meet with us, he did not say much of anything about his investigation. We pressed him further, my family and I, but Armstrong was resolute.

"This was just an unfortunate accident," he finally said, the deepness of his voice conveying a finality on the matter.

That was what he seemed determined to conclude, that no one was at fault in my brother's killing. Just an unfortunate accident. An act of God, if you will. Like trees that fall and destroy houses. Or natural disasters. No one had any control over the situation, especially not Amber Guyger, who made the decision to enter a home and use her gun on an unarmed citizen. Her thoughts were not hers but an act of God.

As my mind returned to the present, I felt that my actions, too, ought to be deemed an act of God. If God would simply will my hand to steer this vehicle over the median and into traffic, then I could find an escape from my daily torment. I all but prayed for this to happen. Nevertheless, I managed to make it home, which meant that God either does not answer prayers or does not hear mine.

* * *

When I entered my house, it was almost 7:00 p.m., more than an hour later than I usually get home. My sons' grandfather was there to greet me. He was my ex-husband's father, but we all referred to him as Grandpa. I could see a lot of him in my sons. Their faces are a little rounder than mine because of him. And their noses flared a bit too. But while their eyes gave their round faces a lightness and joy, his eyes simply looked weary. At times, I found myself looking for a bit of wisdom there, some sense of sagely advice. But shallowness was never seen in such dark-brown eyes as I often saw in his. While I longed for a steady, more sagely presence, his was simply a presence. Nothing more.

"You took a while getting home," he remarked.

"I made a stop," I replied, busying myself with removing my coat and shoes.

"Did you get anything for me?" he said, making an attempted at lightheartedness, but I could hear the impatience in his voice.

"Not this time. Maybe next time."

"That's okay. I'd rather you just get here when you say you're gonna be here."

"Why?" I asked, my eyebrows raised contentiously.

Because I worry when you don't, I wished he would say.

"Because I have things to do too," he replied instead.

"Well, I'm here now. Did the boys eat?"

"They made themselves something."

"Where are they now?"

"Upstairs," he said, standing to retrieve his coat. "I should get going."

"Thank you," I said as he reached the door.

"Mm-hmm," he muttered as he closed the door behind him. Then it was quiet.

My sons were upstairs, and my ex-husband was downstairs in the basement where he had been staying since we separated. I stood in the middle of the living room floor. No food aromas came from the kitchen, for I had put none there. No dining table had been set. The last person to cook for me in this house was Botham. With so much silence and emptiness surrounding me, I thought to sing one of Botham's favorite songs. But I was afraid to have those words break the silence.

You are my strength—

Strength like no other . . .

I could almost hear my brother's voice, and the memory of him singing those words brought me calm. When my smartwatch vibrated, I thought for the briefest of moments that he was returning my phone call from earlier that day. When I looked down at my watch, however, the message that flashed was a warning that my heart rate had risen. It seemed my heart was breaking in that moment, and even my watch knew it.

Determined not to go to bed in a state of despair, I rushed to my room and turned on the television.

Friends.

I had seen every episode, and I knew the reruns would play through the night. I could recite all the characters' lines before they said them. I knew them all well. And I knew everything that would happen in each episode. This meant that there was nothing in them to surprise me. I would not awaken to an unfamiliar scene, no sudden arguments, no tragedies, no gunshots. Bedtime was no time to bother with silence; who knew where my mind would go in my sleep. This was the only time I did not let my mind drift.

The next morning, after I had gotten the boys off to school, I sat quietly in the kitchen and sipped my coffee. I watched the ripples emanate from the center of the cup as one might look at the pebbles in a Zen garden. I realized then that I was shaking, but I was not alarmed. The shaking had been my constant companion since the day of that fateful phone call. It had become familiar, and to think of it as anything other than a reminder to think about Botham never occurred to me.

Later, as I got into my car, I felt calm. In fact, I was almost alarmed by how calm I was.

What right do I have to be relaxed right now? I thought.

Do you need a reason to be relaxed? I replied.

Yes! There is no reason to be relaxed. Everything is wrong.

Everything?

Everything!

These words raced through my mind, and still I felt calm as I put the car in reverse and backed out of the driveway. By the time I'd begun heading down the road, my body was shaking even more than usual. Still, I felt calm. I rolled to the stop sign smoothly and looked both ways through the cross section.

See? You're fine. Look at how well you're handling things?

My watch vibrated. I thought it might be a text message, but I chose not to check it. I was driving, after all, and drivers shouldn't text. Yet the more I thought about it, the more I considered that it might be an important text. Perhaps something was wrong. I pressed the brakes as it occurred to me that maybe one of my sons needed me. But they would call, wouldn't they? I returned my foot to the accelerator and continued down the road. A sudden urge seized me then, and I thought that I must look at the message.

What if it's Botham? What if he needs his sister?

My watch vibrated again, and I thought I should at least take a peek. Slowly, I turned my wrist so I could see it without removing my hand from the steering wheel.

Just a quick peek.

But the watch face did not light up. I had to remove one hand from the steering wheel to tap it. I looked down and saw that the face was still unlit.

Look at the road!

I tapped it twice more, and finally it lit up with the words "Call me, sis!"

It was urgent!

I looked to my bag, where my purse was, and when I looked again at the road, I was blinded by headlights. I closed my eyes and could feel my entire body convulse as I envisioned a gigantic truck crushing me and my car into bits.

When I opened my eyes, I was still in my driveway. I had not even started the car.

But you are so calm.

I looked down at my watch. There was no text message. Only a notification. My heart was racing.

Chapter Six

"You're going to watch the movie with me, right?" Botham asked.

He had visited me the first chance he got during his freshman year at Harding University. I had just purchased a house in Brooklyn, and he was the first of my family to see it. We had a few family members in North Carolina, but otherwise, we were the only family who had and would leave Saint Lucia. Our little brother, Brandt, had remained there, as well as our mother and Bertrum.

I was so proud to have him visit. *We* were so proud to be pursuing an education and better lives in the United States. Still, we felt homesick from time to time, and having Botham in my home helped curb that feeling.

"You won't make it," he teased. "It's too scary."

"Me?" I asked incredulously. "You're the one who can't stand scary movies."

"What?" he asked, his voice rising several octaves. "I love scary movies!"

"I didn't say you didn't. Of course you love them. But you can't stand them. Or sit still when the killer's music comes on. Or sleep after you've watched one. Or stop from crying."

"Oh ho!" he guffawed. "You ain't never seen me crying!"

"You forget I raised you from a baby," I replied with a smirk. "I've seen you cry plenty of times. Seen you wet yourself too."

"When I was a baby."

"No, when you watched *Rosemary's Baby*!"

"Okay, okay," he said. "You have successfully dodged my question. Are you going to watch it with me or what?"

"Sure, I will watch it with you."

"Yes! Get the popcorn!"

"Who says I have popcorn?" I asked

"And the ice cream!"

"Who says I have ice cream?"

"You don't have ice cream?" Botham feigned a gasp of horror. "It's like you don't even know your own brother."

"I'm sorry," I replied. "I just haven't had the chance to go to the store."

"Okay, so go!"

"You're coming with me," I said.

"I'm going to start the movie."

"You're going to start it alone?" I asked.

"Sure."

"Okay."

"What? Do you think I'm scared?"

"I know you are, but I want to support your newfound bravery as best I can. So you go ahead and start the movie, and I'll go get popcorn and ice cream from the store."

"Okay!"

I watched him walk boldly into the living room. The house was empty but for the two of us. My husband was out with the boys, and once I left for the store, he would be alone. In the dark. With *The Conjuring* playing on the television. I watched him for a while longer while he fiddled with the remote control and quite obviously pretended not to notice me. I smiled and headed toward the door.

"Sis!" he called out.

"Yes?"

"How do you work this thing?"

"You're a smart young man. I think you can figure it out."

"Come on! Just find the movie app for me."

I rolled my eyes and joined him in the living room. I put out my hand, indicating that I would help him, but he kept playing with the remote.

"Do you want my help or not?" I asked.

"Not," he replied.

"Then why did you call me over here?"

"Because I thought I needed help, but I think I got it now."

I turned to leave the room, but he called me back. "Is it under *C* for conjuring or *T* for the?"

"Bye!" I said.

"Wait!" he called. "I haven't even started the movie."

"You can start it when I'm gone."

"No! It's way scarier like that."

"So what do you want me to do?"

"Just wait until I get it started."

I leaned against the doorway while he searched the movie titles. He took his sweet time getting to the title, and I was amused the entire time. Once he found it, I turned to leave again.

"Wait!"

"What, Bo?"

"Do you have any kind of snacks? I can't start the movie without at least something."

"You can go in the kitchen and find it," I replied.

"And where will you be?"

"In the car going to the store."

"So you're just going to let me walk into the kitchen and then walk all the way back alone?"

"What are you afraid of?"

"I'm not afraid," he said with a smirk. "I'm just . . . well . . . sensitive."

"Boy, go in there and get your snacks!" I tried to speak in a stern tone, but I could not hold back a chuckle.

"You'll wait?" he asked.

"I'll wait."

"You promise."

"I'm right here."

He selected the movie but paused it before he went into the kitchen and found some berries in the refrigerator and chips in a cabinet. Once he sat down, I got far enough away to open the front door.

"Wait!" he called. I closed the door, feigning frustration. "I have to use the bathroom."

I burst out laughing at this point. He was nearly six feet tall and as broad in the chest as an ox. And he was telling me he had to go potty in the softest voice he could manage.

"Do you even want ice cream?" I asked.

"Yes," he replied. "But later."

"How much later?"

"Just watch the start of the movie with me."

We had played this game often, and it never ceased to amuse me. Botham loved horror movies, but he never wanted to watch them alone. As he grew older and bigger, he would watch them alone, but he could not walk around the house before or after watching them unless he turned on all of the lights in the house. It helped if I was there. He would get everything he thought he would need so that when I left, he wouldn't have to get up and walk around the house. Whatever monster was in the movie might be lurking in the dark.

On that night, I never made it out of the house to get the ice cream and popcorn. I stayed with him and watched the whole movie.

I'm right here.

Chapter Seven

It would have been easy to pretend that Botham's death never happened. Even before the first funeral in Dallas, before we buried him in Saint Lucia, I had considered it. From the moment I got the call from Baylor University Medical Center, I think the idea had always been in the back of my mind. At both funerals, I found myself coming up with ways to convince myself that I was not truly at his funeral, that Botham was alive and well somewhere in the world. When I sat at his funeral service in Dallas, I began to imagine that he was just back home for a visit to Saint Lucia. And that's when I remembered his brother.

Valdez, I thought. *I could bring him here.*

Valdez was my half-brother, Botham's full brother. The two could have been twins. I did not know Valdez as well as I should have, but when I was suddenly faced with life without Botham, I wished I had been closer to him. I wanted to be closer to him.

He could not fill the hole in my heart. But maybe his presence could help distract me. Or maybe I could just pretend Botham was not really gone. He could be Botham. Couldn't You do that, Lord? Couldn't You just make him Botham? Even for a little while?

I would have to teach him about football. Or maybe he could learn to play rugby the way Bo did. The more I thought about it, the more I thought it could work.

I remained seated in the church pews for a long while after the Dallas service was done. I didn't even notice the woman approaching me with sympathetic eyes. I had recognized her at the beginning of the service as someone who worked with Botham. Her expression was the most somber of all the others. She wore a black dress with layers that made her look as though she were clothed in a trash bag.

"You look so sad," she remarked as she sat down at my table. I did not want to say anything to her. I just wanted to be alone with my thoughts, to figure out my plan. But then the woman sat down and forced me to focus on the reality. She was a young, slender woman with blonde hair and a gentle smile. She had introduced herself by saying that Botham was her person.

Was.

"If you want to cry, that is natural," she said.

I knew that. I did not need this stranger to tell me that. Furthermore, I did not *want* her to tell me that. Botham *is my* person, and I wasn't in any particular mood to share that distinction. Of course, I admired that so many thought that of him. So many of his friends from Harding were in attendance. He had lifted their voices in the choir, brought out their competitive spirits in rugby games, and inspired their ambitions in the classroom and in the office. Everyone felt like Botham was their person. But in that moment, I wished he had made fewer friends.

"You look so terribly sad," the young woman continued. "It's okay to smile."

I don't want to smile.

I do not know if I scowled or made any other expression that would signal I didn't want her or anyone's company. Nevertheless, she stood up and walked away, back into the reception crowd to bug someone else.

Now where was I? Oh yes. Valdez. He smiles like Botham. Maybe he is just as kind. And generous.

The last time Botham and I had spent his birthday together was last year. I had brought him up to New York to surprise him and celebrate with him. I'd even considered cooking for him. However, before I could give him my gift, even before he had hardly said hello, he was asking me to drive him to Best Buy. There, he made a beeline for the electronics section and became very busy with the sales reps. Before long, he was packing a flat-screen television in the trunk of my car.

"And who is that for?" I asked.

"You!" he said with squinted eyes and a wide grin that revealed brilliantly white teeth.

"Me?" I asked, bewildered.

"Yes!"

"But it isn't my birthday."

"Does it need to be your birthday for a brother to do something nice for his sister.

"No, but it is quite literally your birthday. I'm supposed to be buying you something. You're just tired of watching movies on my computer when you come over," I said.

"Sure," he said, grinning again. "That too."

I hugged him and marveled at how big he had become. Hugging him was like putting my arms around a tree, and I had to reach up if I wanted to get my arms around his neck.

"Thank you," I said into his chest as he hugged me back.

Why does a man like that not deserve his life. He deserves life more than I do. Even more than Valdez. What man was more devoted to You, God?

"Cheer up." The woman with the frumpy black dress was at my table and smiling down at me.

"What?" I said, my blood boiling and the heat rising and settling about my collar. I was certain I had turned some shade of red.

"Cheer up," she repeated. "Botham would have wanted to see you smile."

The anger rose in my chest so that my heart pounded and my heavy breaths rushed from my lungs and burst out of my ears. I slammed my hand down and stood to look her directly in the eyes.

"Don't tell me what Botham would have wanted!" I shouted. "And don't tell me what to do with *my* face."

The woman's skin turned white as a sheet, and she seemed to drift away in her trash-bag dress. Perhaps that had not been the nicest way to handle that situation, but at least I knew she would not be back.

But in that moment, I felt I had made my case to God. Botham would have never shown anger that way. He would have been more patient. He would have returned the woman's sympathy. No one had to tell Botham to cheer up. Even on his darkest days, he found a way to be strong and find a reason to smile. He was good. Why take someone like him from this earth? There are more than enough people like me around.

I listened to the expressed condolences from many more strangers before I was finally able to retreat to the stairwell. I hid there, listening for signs that people were leaving the service and heading home. My mother and Botham's father, Bertrum, had come, as well as my little brother, Brandt, and Aunt Desma.

Valdez was not here, and the more I thought about my plan, the more ridiculous it sounded. I wanted to talk to Botham, to hear his advice again, to have my confidant back. Although the brothers looked so much alike, the one could never take the other's place. Valdez and I hardly knew each other. How could I possibly pretend that he was Botham. It had always been a crazy idea, but for a brief moment I thought I had come up with a perfect plan. I would have to think of some other way to keep Botham alive.

I tried today. I'll try again tomorrow.

Chapter Eight

I had not meant to laugh. But there was so much joy in their voices. Two months after his death, this was the first Thanksgiving holiday I would spend without Botham. I usually celebrated Thanksgiving at my house with family, but I could not bear to do that this year. So we were driving to a hotel in Tribeca.

My oldest, Jayden, sat in the front seat beside me as we drove down the road and away from home. He twisted his body in the seat, stretching his seat belt so he could look back at his younger brother, Jareem, with a wide and knowing grin.

"What do you call a can opener that doesn't work?" Jayden asked.

"I don't know," Jareem replied.

"A can't opener!" Jayden said, squealing with laughter. In the rearview mirror, I saw Jareem roll his eyes, though I suspected he liked the joke and only wished he'd cracked the punch line.

"It wasn't that funny," Jareem mumbled. Then he perked up in the seat. "Okay, my turn. What do you call an alligator in a vest?"

"An investigator!" Jayden howled, proud of his cleverness.

"You heard that one before," Jareem accused him.

"No, I didn't," Jayden responded. "I'm just clever like that."

"Okay then. I have another one."

"Go ahead," Jayden said confidently. "I'll just figure that one out too."

"No you won't," Jareem said.

"Yes, I will."

"No, you won't."

"Yes, I will!" Jayden had stifled his laughter, but he still wore a smirk. By that time, I'd become curious to hear what Jareem could possibly say to stump his brother, who was older and, indeed, more clever. Deep down, I was rooting for my younger son.

"Ready?" Jareem asked.

"Go right ahead," Jayden said smugly.

"Why don't dinosaurs talk?" Jareem asked. The smile slowly faded from Jayden's face as he pondered the question. I looked in the rearview mirror to see that it was Jareem who was now grinning knowingly at his big brother. There was a long silence before Jayden attempted an answer.

"Maybe..." Jayden began, dragging out the word to give himself more time. "Maybe because..."

"Give up?" Jareem teased, sensing that he had his brother on the ropes.

"No," Jayden replied, but his clipped tone told a different story.

"Give up," Jareem said with a sigh. He was losing patience, and he began to squirm and fidget in his seat. His grin grew wider because he knew that his brother didn't know the answer.

"Fine," Jayden relented.

"Because they're dead!" Jareem declared.

Initially, I coughed to clear my throat, but once the sound escaped, the laughter came pouring out. At first, both boys just looked at me, but Jareem soon joined in the laughter, and then Jayden began to chuckle.

I do not know what the source of my laughter was. The joke was hardly even a joke, and the solution was curt and unironic. Yet I laughed long and hard. I almost didn't recognize the sound; it was the first laugh out of my mouth in the entire two months since

Botham had passed.

Perhaps it was simply that my younger son had finally bested his older brother, and I could feel Jareem's sense of satisfaction in his laughter. Maybe I hadn't expected Jareem to be so curt. Nor had I expected that any of us would be laughing at the word *dead*. Not so soon. It was this revelation that caused me to abruptly stop laughing even as Jayden and Jareem continued with their game.

I had not meant to laugh. I had no right to. I had become too comfortable too soon; it had only been two months since Botham died.

That's right! I thought. *You left me. Did you expect that I would never laugh again?* Immediately, I felt terrible.

I'm so sorry! Of course it wasn't your fault. I should have been there. I should have been there to save you. It must have been so awful for you to die that way: alone, with no loved one to mark the occasion or see you on into the next life. I am truly sorry, my dear brother.

"I don't want to play this game anymore," Jareem whined. I had not been listening to their conversation, so I hadn't noticed that it had become more teasing than competition. Nevertheless, I was bothered by both of their tones.

"Oh, don't get mad at me because you're too slow to figure it out," Jayden jeered. "Don't hate on me because I'm clever."

"Stop it!" I snapped at them both, but especially Jayden. "That's your brother. You're supposed to take care of each other."

"Are we almost there?" Jareem interjected.

"Did you hear me?" I said. "Be good to each other."

"Yes, Mom," they said in unison. Their agreement calmed me for a second.

My watch had started vibrating, but I had an idea of what it was. I did not need or want to confirm it.

"Are we there yet?" Jareem repeated.

"Almost," I said.

Botham usually came up from Dallas to cook and spend time with us during the Thanksgiving holiday. I looked forward to the family time, but I especially looked forward to Botham's cooking. If I could have found an excuse that would convince him to make chicken Alfredo every Thanksgiving, I would have. I asked him every year, and he always said no. But he would also promise to make it on another visit, and I would hold him to that promise; his recipe was always so good.

For Thanksgiving, I always made him lasagna. It was his favorite. Of course, there would be no mention of chicken Alfredo this Thanksgiving. And he could not be there to eat my lasagna. So I had no desire to make it. And I had no desire to be in a kitchen where I would be very tempted to make it. Instead, I packed bags for my sons and me, and we headed to a fancy hotel in Manhattan. I supposed this was the start of a new holiday tradition.

Still, as we arrived at the hotel, I was determined not to laugh again; laughter was a betrayal to Botham. But my sons seemed to have other ideas.

"Can you do this dance?" Jareem asked me as he moved rhythmically to a song that only he could hear. His elbows straight and his hands balled into fists, he shook his hips and moved his arms back and forth by his sides. He looked ridiculous, but his face was so serious, I smiled in spite of myself.

"What in the world is that?" I asked, holding back a chuckle.

"Flossing," he replied.

"That ain't no flossing I ever heard of," I said. "I thought that was something you did with your teeth."

"No!" he said. "That's a different kind. This way is much cooler."

"Do you see yourself?" I asked.

"Can you do it?" Jayden chimed in.

"I won't even try," I said. "That ain't no kind of dancing I ever heard of."

"She can't do it," Jayden said matter-of-factly. He and Jareem laughed, so I made the attempt. It wasn't that difficult.

"None of your dances are difficult," I remarked. "Now our dances? Those were hard."

"Like what?" Jareem asked.

"Well, for starters, we used music," I teased as I got my phone and found a song. Before long, we were dancing and laughing.

Laughing.

"Okay, I'm tired now," I said after a few minutes, hoping they would continue on without me.

Occupied by their music and dance, they did not notice that I'd retreated to the bathroom and quietly closed the door behind me. When I looked in the mirror, I discovered that the smile had not yet left my face. It slowly faded with the discovery.

There is a feeling children get when they have done something wrong, when they know they are in trouble. A sinking feeling down in the pit of their stomach. You know when you get home, you are going to be punished. And even if you forget in the middle of the day, it always comes back to you, usually in the moments you are the most hopeful. Maybe you have fun at recess or you start to look forward to lunch or dinner. But then it dawns on you that you're going to be punished soon. I have felt this way every day since Botham was killed.

You rarely get that feeling as an adult because you are rarely in such trouble. You'd have to commit a crime to feel such dread. I imagine the moment when a thief is caught, he knows that his immediate future is doomed. I've read books where murderers are doomed to a lifetime of mental anguish over the murders they committed. But those are just fictional characters in books. I like to think that whenever a prisoner wakes up from a good dream, they are deeply saddened to return to their reality. That is how I felt dancing with my sons that day.

I wonder if Amber Guyger has good dreams. I hope she doesn't. I hope her guilt feels like my grief.

But you are guilty too? Aren't you? I asked myself.

Am I?

You are. He died alone. Whose fault is that?

How is it mine?

Are you your brother's keeper?

I am.

Then you know whose fault it is.

But I didn't pull the trigger.

No, you didn't. But what if you could have been there? Would that cop have even entered Botham's home if you were in there? Maybe he needed you to close that door all the way.

"Bullshit. I don't even believe that door was open."

Do you have proof it wasn't?

"I don't need proof. I know it wasn't open."

But you don't know. You weren't there. But you should have been.

"I should have been there."

But you weren't, were you?

"I was not."

And look what happened because you weren't there. Another racist cop shot another Black man. And this wasn't just any Black man. This was your baby brother. She broke into your baby brother's home and shot him dead.

"Another racist cop . . ."

Or maybe not. Maybe she was just scared like she said.

"She was scared?"

You don't know. You weren't there.

"I wasn't there."

But you should have been. He was your person, wasn't he?

"He was my person."

But he died alone. I bet that cop had a bunch of her friends by her side to console her. But who did Botham have?

"No one."

He should have had you.

"He should have."

So you are guilty, aren't you? Your guilt feels like grief because guilt is grief.

"No!"

No?

"What I feel and what that cop feels are not the same thing."

No, it is exactly the same. You both feel awful. You both had very different ideas for what you would be doing now. The only difference is the police officer has a chance at redemption; she can be absolved of this feeling. You will have to live with what she did all your life.

"She won't live with what she did?"

She doesn't have to. She didn't lose a life; she took one. And if you think she will lose sleep over that any longer than it takes to beat the case, you're a new fool. She doesn't even know what was lost. You know the whole person. She knew a silhouette. She quite literally saw his Blackness and nothing else.

"I should have been there. He should not have been alone."

And yet, he was.

"So I am guilty."

Guilty as original sin.

"And I shouldn't laugh?"

Only if you are happy when you do it. Are you happy?

"How can I be?"

A knock at the door startled me out of my thoughts.

"Mom?" Jayden called. "Are you okay?"

"I am," I replied from behind the closed bathroom door.

"Who are you talking to?" Jareem asked.

"I'm on a call," I said.

"How? Your phone is in my hand."

"Calling on the Lord," I said.

That wasn't far from the truth. God is always listening, isn't He?

Chapter Nine

Sometimes anger is good. It opens the eyes and moves the blood. Anger is natural. Things should make you mad; that's how you know you care about them. Therefore sometimes anger is good. As long as the feeling is fleeting. Never let it linger.

You should never allow anger to linger because when that happens, it spreads. And when anger spreads, it starts to feel good. Really good. And that good feeling, that euphoria means you should have let that anger go a long time ago. Because in a very short while, all of that good will start to feel like you are burning alive.

It had been fourteen months since Botham's death, and the anger that had dug its roots into me felt *so* good. But not like warm-sunshine-and-mango-on-a-summer-day good. Not like a hug from your grandma or clean sheets on your skin after a shower. Anger doesn't feel good like that.

Anger feels like scratching a mosquito bite, scraping away at your own skin but soothing a most troublesome ailment. Before long, the itch is gone and only the burn remains. And maybe a little blood.

Even though you may scratch with a fervent sense of vengeance, the mosquito doesn't feel your scratching. Neither does it feel your scraping nor your burning. Only you feel those things. And still you scratch like you're somehow getting back at the thing that bit you, the thing that took your blood from your body and then went on about the rest of her life.

But anger also sets in like a mosquito bite—the female, of course. She comes in ever so concerned with her life and what she will make of it. And she drinks blood with no concern for the person who loses it. Sometimes you don't even realize the mosquito has taken your blood until you've been scratching at her bite for too long. Then it is too late; your skin has already swelled and the mosquito has already moved on to other parts of your body.

That is how that first phone call to my mother felt, like a bite I'd scratched before I knew what it was. By the time I was watching Amber Guyger cry her eyes out before a jury, so full of sorrow for the life she was about to lose but not for the life she had taken, I was itching all over.

"I was by myself with someone I just shot . . ." she said through sobs. "I was alone with him, and that's the scariest thing you can ever imagine." She spoke so very remorsefully to her attorney, and I sat there and listened.

No, that is not the scariest thing I can imagine, I thought as I slowly moved my hand down my crossed legs, closer and closer to the foot within closest reach.

Her words had settled in my left ankle, in that space between the bone and the Achilles tendon, and I began to rub there almost absentmindedly as I listened to her sniveling voice and watched her eyes bulge from the red and sunken hollows of their sockets.

Or maybe you're right, Officer. Maybe he didn't even have time to get to a scarier place than you can imagine. Maybe death always comes before some people can get there.

Or perhaps Guyger could not fathom the nightmare that I was going through, the nightmare that my entire family was living.

The trial had been going on for five days, and in that time, we'd had to withstand the criminalization of Botham. Although it was Guyger who entered Botham's home, the defense constantly referred to his apartment as Guyger's apartment. Hearing Guyger on the stand refer to the place as "my apartment" made me want to scream. She had not been at her home; she'd had no reason to fear for her life. Botham did. But no one ever thinks that a Black person can imagine something scarier.

For a Black man, the scariest idea isn't that he will be shot down by a police officer even if he is innocent. The scariest thing he can imagine is that he will be shot down and his innocence will *never* be discovered. And that was what the Dallas Police Department was trying to do in the trial. They were not trying to get to the bottom of Botham's murder; they were trying to get to the top of Guyger's innocence. Because if the apartment was Guyger's, as everyone on her side continued to say throughout the trial, then Botham was guilty of being a burglar. But even if it were his apartment, then they wanted him to be guilty of being in the wrong place at the wrong time. He was a menacing presence for the poor White woman.

"And I just wanted help," Guyger continued. "I wanted someone there."

So did he.

I could not understand her tears. I mean, I understood tears. I had my own. I had been drowning in my mother's and my aunt's tears. But our tears and hers were not the same. Ours were for Botham, for the loss of another human being who meant so very much to us. And as we sat in that courtroom, our tears were for something more; they were for a justice we were all but certain Botham would not get. I was not yet sure who Guyger's tears were for.

"I was scared," Guyger said, sniffling.

So was he.

"(And I'm sorry). And I have to live with that every single day."

But he won't live another day at all.

I could hear the parenthesis in her apology. It seemed like an afterthought, as though she had to remind herself to say what we wanted to hear along with everything she needed to say as she looked pitifully at the jury.

My fingernails tore at the skin by my ankle, around it, and then all over the swelling that rose there. Then my hand drifted up to the back of my neck. I felt what could have been nothing more than a pimple, and I traced my fingernails around it. Slowly, at first. But my God, did it itch! As I circled that bump, it slowly began to swell. Before long, I could not help digging my fingernails right into the middle of it.

My dearest Bo, why couldn't you live? Why couldn't you hang on? To hell with her training and her failure to administer CPR—to do her damned job, to serve and protect! You should've hung on anyway. In spite of her. To spite her.

"I hate that I have to live with this." Guyger sniffled again.

What you *have to live with?*

The skin on the back of my neck broke. I could feel it burning, and still the air suddenly felt cool there.

Our tears are not the same. My tears are for our loss. Yours are for your loss. You have lost something, haven't you? Even if you are trying your damnedest to keep it right now in front of a judge, a jury, and all of your victims.

"I had this *guy* lying on the floor," Guyger uttered.

This guy? Botham! Botham Jean! Say his name, goddamn you! You had Botham Jean *lying on the floor!*

"I never want anybody to have to go through or even imagine having to go through what I went through that night," Guyger concluded, shifting her glance from her attorney to the jury and back again.

What she went through.

My hand drifted to the back of my leg, right behind my knee, the best place for itches. As I traced the new swelling there, I realized that this woman—so contrite as she was, so afflicted by the crime she had committed against the "guy" lying on the floor—could not bring herself to cry actual tears. Her face was dry as bone. And then I remembered there was a long period of time when I did not cry either.

But our dry eyes are not the same. Neither she nor I could shed tears, but the difference is this: She can't cry because she has no real tears to shed. I couldn't cry because my tears might have drowned me.

As our prosecutors began to question her, I noticed a burning sensation all over my body. My fingers traveled from my ankle, to my knee, to my neck, then back to my ankle as I scratched itches and set fires.

I noticed many things about the way Guyger spoke and moved on the witness stand, but chief among these was that she no longer feigned tears. Talking to her attorneys, it seemed she knew exactly when to screw up her face and shed tears. When cross-examined, though, all of her remorse completely left the courtroom. I had to keep myself from standing and screaming at her. So I focused on the itching. And the stinging. And the burning.

As I closed my eyes and tried to drown out her voice, my mind wandered to the phone call I'd had with my mother when we found out about Botham's death.

"His birthday would have been this month," she said with a whimper.

"It still will be," I replied, but she did not seem to hear me.

"Weren't you going to get him those concert tickets?" she asked. I had been planning to buy him Drake tickets for the performance in Dallas just a day before his birthday.

I am going to buy those tickets, I thought. I would have said it aloud, but my mother began wailing again. I wanted to console her, but I could not. Although I wanted to raise my voice, to say something abrasive, I waited in silence for her cries to subside on their own. She only stopped when another thought occurred to her.

"I'll have to tell Brandt," she said soberly. "I don't know if I can do that."

"You don't have to," I replied.

"What do you mean? Of course I have to."

"You don't."

"I do."

"You don't!" I didn't realize how hard I had been breathing until the sound filled the room.

"Why do you yell at me?" she said quietly.

"Because . . ." I paused to sigh. "You don't have to tell Brandt. You don't have to tell anyone."

"What is wrong with you?" she replied. "Of course I do."

"You don't! You don't have to say anything."

"But Botham is dead."

"You don't know that!" I shouted. "Why does that have to be true? Because somebody on the other side of a phone said it?"

"Silly girl!" my mother replied.

"No! You're silly. You believe everything people say? Well I know Botham better than anyone. They're not gonna tell me what my brother is. He's my brother!"

"Dear girl," my mother said. "I know it's hard. I don't want to accept it either."

"Then why do you?" I asked. "Why do you believe it so easily. It hasn't even been an hour since we got the call, and already you believe what they said about him. You're already planning life without him."

"What do you mean?" she asked. "What plan?"

"His birthday *is* in a few weeks," I said. "And I *am* buying him the concert tickets."

"But dear," my mother said sympathetically, "he won't go."

I did not respond. Instead, I let the silence linger and grow until it filled the chasm between my mother all the way in Saint Lucia and me in New York.

"I have to go," I whispered. Then I hung up before she could start crying again. The silence only filled the room now.

* * *

One, two, three, four, five. Five mosquito bites in October. I hate Texas.

I opened my eyes to see Guyger's pitiful face. Then the silence faded, and I could hear her sniveling.

"This is not about hate," Guyger said. "It's about being scared."

Yes, Guyger, you are correct about that. Hatred and fear. *Two sides of the same racist coin.*

Chapter Ten

Anger is a strange thing to have inside you when you're at church; they don't mix well. By the end of the trial, anger was no longer an itch but an outright fever without a remedy. There was no longer a need to scratch, only a strong desire to spread the fever elsewhere and everywhere. I even brought anger into the church. Doing so had become a guilty pleasure, especially on days when members of our congregation listened to my cries and watched the tears stream down my face for entire church services, only to approach me afterward and forget to ask about me.

"How is your mother?" they would ask.

"She is as good as she can be," I usually responded. "Of course, things have been quite hard on her."

"I'll keep her in my prayers," they often said. "And how about Brandt?" Those who knew me often asked about my little brother. I loved Brandt, but our being twenty years apart meant that we did not speak as often as Botham and I spoke. He and Botham were much closer, and losing Botham was very hard on Brandt.

"He hasn't spoken much," I often said about my youngest brother. He had always been a meeker soul.

"Keep an eye on your youngest brother," some members of the church would advise me. "The quiet ones never let you know when they're suffering. We'll keep him in our prayers."

"Of course," I always replied.

Whenever I had these encounters with church members, I felt the angriest. But I was not upset by the questions that were asked; I was angered by the ones that were not.

"Allisa, how are you doing?" I wanted to hear. "Are you hanging in there?"

"Yes," I might have said, simply to be polite. Or I might have told them how I was truly doing. I might have, but I didn't. Why? Because no one ever asked me how *I* was doing.

Perhaps the people I knew were used to me taking care of others and making them feel at home or less hungry or less anxious. The same people took for granted that I was okay, that I would be okay. They never considered that I might be burning up inside. I needed the support of my congregation like medicine for my malady. But I never felt more alone than when I was at church. I don't even know that I felt the presence of God there. And that was strange because until Botham died, I always knew where God was. He was everywhere. He was with me in my time of need and my time of happiness. He was omnipotent and omnipresent. Whether I called on Him or not, I felt that He watched over me. What reason had I to ever wonder if He were there when I needed Him? But then, I needed Him to keep Botham alive, and He hadn't. There could be no greater loss than losing Botham, so what need had I for God?

You need Him until the end of the trial.

And after?

I don't know, I thought as we drove to the courthouse. *I guess it depends on this verdict.*

Will you stop believing in God if He doesn't give you what you want?

No. That's not it. But it will be hard to understand why He took Botham if the murderer gets away with it.

You know that's not how it works, right?

I know.

Faith isn't there for when you understand.

I know.

Faith is there for when you don't understand.

I know.

Just like religion isn't there to keep bad things from happening.

Then what is it there for?

To console you when bad things happen.

And what am I to think of why things happen?

Nothing.

Nothing?

Faith isn't for understanding the why.

But things happen for a reason, don't they? Or am I to believe what the Texas Ranger believes? That no one is to blame for Botham's murder?

Is that the same thing?

I don't know. Is it?

As we approached the court building for the verdict, I looked up at the brick edifice that stretched high toward the sky and spread far along the horizon. It seemed to approach me while I stood still. Although the entire building was bisected by an immense lobby made entirely of glass, that glass only made the brick sections, with their tiny windows, appear more menacing.

We parked and headed across the parking lot to the courthouse. I could not even stand to look at the South Side Flats where Botham was killed. Yet I'd had to walk into this building every day of the week-long trial. Going never got easier.

The walk to the main entrance felt eternal, so I began to look around to my family, in part for comfort but more so to ensure that this was really happening, that we were finally reaching the verdict for Botham's killer more than a year after his murder.

Bertrum's face and my mother's bore a solemnity, which I expected. Brandt's face, however, was blank, and I was not sure what to think of this. Until today, it seemed that the loss of our brother had weighed on him the most. Although he had always been quiet and that had not changed, a darkness was born in him the day of the murder, one he had seemed to be nurturing into a most violent monster over the year leading up to the trial.

Once, during a Sunday service that was particularly difficult for me, I saw Brandt manifest that monster in the most unsettling way.

The choir was singing a stirring a cappella rendition of "You Are My Strength." I loved to hear Botham sing that song, so with every note that came from their mouths, I felt weaker and weaker. Beside me, Brandt must have been similarly affected because he began to shake. Then he rocked back and forth. By the time the tears began to well up in his eyes, they were already streaming from mine. The moment I felt the wail forming in my throat, Brandt suddenly jerked back against the pew. With immense power, his fist thrust forward and crashed into the pew in front of us. The sound was nearly drowned out by the choir, but when his other first crashed into the pew, its sound almost silenced the choir. He struck the pew a third time before I wrapped my arms around him and held on for dear life.

Botham's dear life . . .

The choir wavered at first but continued their song as Brandt and I drowned in each other's tears.

That was, perhaps, the most passionate outburst I had ever seen from Brandt in the eighteen years he had been on this earth. But a visit to my mother's house before the first funeral revealed to me that his anger was as fervent as mine: the walls, especially those in his room, were riddled with fist-sized holes.

With the memory of that church service in mind, I walked with my family toward the courthouse and found some comfort when I looked at Brandt's hands and saw remnants of bruises around his knuckles. Perhaps he would pound the entire building into the ground if I needed him to.

We took our usual seats on the bench to the left of the testimony stand. From our seats, I could look across the room and get an unfettered view of Guyger. Her appearance had changed many times from the first day of the trial. Back then, her hair was pulled back and she wore a frumpy shirt and dark pants that I thought paired well with her stern expression. She had come across as a severe woman with a face perfectly capable of having once said, "I wear all black to remind you not to mess with me because I'm already dressed for your funeral."

By the day of the verdict, her fashion choices had softened. She wore her hair down and had added blonde highlights that made you think of streams of light. Her clothing included much lighter shades than she had worn at the beginning of the trial. Her sweater was a pale shade of purple, and her skirt was tight enough to suggest a figure but close enough to the knee to tell you that she was traditionally feminine. She could have been any of the women with whom Botham had worked and who had held him in such high esteem. But her face still said, "No one ever thanks me for having the patience not to kill them. People are so ungrateful."

As I looked at her on that day, I wondered if she had been drugged during the trial. I wished that I could say she was so overcome with grief over having killed an innocent man that she had been rendered catatonic. But when she made the 911 call after his murder, when she sat in the car texting her married lover as Botham's body was being whisked away before her, and when she took the witness stand to give her account of that night, she expressed an overwhelming concern for herself and her career; her concern for Botham's life always seemed like an afterthought.

If only you could have held on a bit longer, Bo. Would you understand my vexation if you could see how your killer sits there, worrying about her life after she has taken yours? Would you understand why I want to shake her?

Guyger sat so perfectly still that for a minute I imagined her to be a mere corpse propped up by the ghosts of the first policemen in the American South: slave patrollers who enforced the eighteenth- and nineteenth-century Black Codes and the twentieth-century Jim Crow law enforcers who took their place.

It was only when the judge entered, when she was required to stand at the behest of the most powerful person in the room—a

Black woman—that I again became aware that Amber Guyger was very much alive, and that her real-life existence as a former police officer had started just two decades after the end of Jim Crow. Her mother had lived through that era in Texas. I wondered what kind of stories she'd passed on to her daughter. Or if she taught her daughter to worship the same God.

Did she learn to trust in You the way I'd learned? Did she pray to You like I did? Is she praying now?

As these thoughts played in my head, my body shook, as it had for most of the past year. It was not cold in the room; in fact, it felt quite the opposite. But that is what sicknesses do to the body; they make it fight the affliction within. And I was so afflicted with anger that I could not take my eyes off Guyger, even after the judge asked us to be seated.

She prays for innocence, I thought. *She wants this court to tell her what it has told almost every police officer who has sat in this building since it was built: you are right. Right to take someone's life. Even an innocent life. I cannot speak for every life that has been taken by the law, but I can certainly speak for Botham's. He wasn't in the wrong place at the wrong time. He wasn't in the wrong at all. He was in the most innocent place at the most innocent time. So when is it right to take a most innocent life?*

We had not been seated long before the judge asked Guyger and her attorneys to stand again. She read the verdict promptly, but for me, there seemed to be an eternity between each word so that it seemed as if the entire lifetime that I lived with my faith flashed before my eyes.

"We, the jury . . ."

I, Allisa Charles-Findley, who has been a devoted child of God since I could open my mouth, who has sung Your praises and followed Your Word, but who has faltered in this trying time...

". . . unanimously find the defendant . . ."

. . . do humbly promise that I can do better. That I will do better. I may not understand Your will, but I can do better to understand

that You do not give me anything You do not think I can handle, that there is a higher purpose to all of this, that Botham's death will not be in vain. All I ask is that You give me some sign now...

"... guilty of murder..."

When the judge spoke those words, my mother made an audible gasp that made my fever jump out of my body. I felt a sudden warmth all over, and in that moment, my shaking stopped. My mother stood and raised her hands to the sky.

Chapter Eleven

The sentencing, on the other hand, was quite different. I had prayed for a just verdict. I'd forgotten to pray for a just sentence. Of course, I'd had a number in mind. It was greater than the number that came from the judge's mouth.

"Ten years," she announced.

When I thought of that number in relation to the years Amber Guyger had taken from Botham, the entire courtroom fell away. I was no longer in Texas.

Tropical breezes brushed my cheek. I could faintly smell the ocean on the breeze. But I couldn't see the ocean. In fact, I couldn't see anything. It was dark, but I could hear my mother and father sobbing. Being at the sentencing was like watching my brother be buried all over again. And the words that the pastor said at Botham's funeral were playing again in my mind:

". . . and although the circumstances are not ideal, are indeed tragic, we can take some solace in knowing that our Botham is going home to be with the Lord now."

For a moment, I thought my eyes were simply closed, so I tried to open them. But I was no longer in the courtroom. The darkness would not give way to light. I thought to rub my eyes, but my hands remained glued to my sides. I strained to lift my hands, tried to flex my arms, and finally I sought to shrug my shoulders. But my body was imperturbably still. I heard the sound, simultaneously close and far away, of metal being thrust into dirt. Then I heard the clump of that dirt falling somewhere in front of my face. It was then that

I realized I was neither sitting nor standing. I was lying straight, and although the dirt was falling somewhere right above my face, it never touched me.

My mother sobbed nearby as the dirt fell just in front of my face, then on my body and on my legs. When I finally heard a third voice cry out, I was puzzled by its familiarity.

"Don't!" the voice cried. "He's afraid of the dark!"

I was both alarmed by this voice and comforted by the air of importance and justice in it. The voice reasoned to someone, and as the voice grew closer, I realized why the voice was familiar. It was mine.

The voice grew closer and closer until there was a sudden thud in front of me as well as a sound like someone sweeping dirt away. Then a glimmer of light peeked into what I could see as some sort of room with walls that were disturbingly close to me. It occurred to me then that I was in a prison of some sort, and this person with my voice was trying to free me!

Hurry, I thought. I was becoming frantic from the realization that I was imprisoned.

I am here! I thought. *And I am so desperately afraid of this place!*

"Get him out of there!" I heard myself shout though my lips remained closed. The glimmer of light grew until it spread over the entire room. Then, before one wall fell away and the Saint Lucian sky was before me, I saw that the walls were entirely adorned in white satin. I tried to reach toward the sky, but my body remained still.

Finally, I saw a face before me that ought to have caused my heart to seize up in my chest. I looked upon my own face, and it was more distraught and tear-soaked than I had ever known it could be. My eyes and hers became the same in that moment, and I looked down at Botham in his coffin. My mother and father, along with Brandt, came to my side to carry me away from the coffin. A pallbearer closed it. When my family returned me to my seat, I closed my eyes and became still for a long time.

When I opened my eyes, I was in the courtroom again. Brandt, my aunt, and Valdez were closest to me, but before long they were standing to leave the courtroom. I remained seated on the bench, and I felt my aunt place her hand on my shoulder.

Ten years, I thought. *For murder. That's all his life was worth? Ten years?*

Slowly, I bowed my head and cradled it in my hands. The tears flowed into my palms and the shaking returned.

Earlier that day, the judge had asked if any members of our family wanted to give a victim impact statement. We had all declined. We felt no need to provide any kind of closure to Amber Guyger. We were all in accord on this. Except Brandt.

Brandt Jean, who had been the quietest of us all throughout the trial, decided that he would speak, that he would choose words to express to Amber Guyger what she had taken from him—from all of us.

When I saw that he had volunteered to do so, I was quite surprised. I could not, for the life of me, figure out what possessed him to do it. We did not know he intended to do so, and it was quite outside of his character. I don't think he knew before the moment that he was going to say anything at all. In fact, it may have been Brandt's grandmother who'd influenced him to do anything at all. When the judge asked if any of us had anything we wished to express to Guyger during the sentencing, no sound had arisen from our benches; nobody had stirred. Then Brandt's grandmother had whispered something into the silence that had only fallen on a few ears.

"But what about her soul?" his grandmother had asked.

Suddenly, our courtroom benches had become church pews, and I felt that I was at the benediction of what had been an impossibly long service and an especially difficult sermon—one of those sermons that draws upon the guilt of indulging the natural pleasures: those of material wealth, those of the flesh, those of the heart. I was quite content to ignore this call to the altar. Even though

I could feel the tug in my heart the way I had felt it in my youth, I told myself I was not the one in need of God's grace on that day. But I did recall the first time I'd felt this tug at my heart, the first time I had been compelled to go up to the altar.

* * *

"But the light provides your opportunity to come back to Jesus, who is the Light," the minister had said. "So if you feel that you may have strayed, you can always come back to the light. Stay in the light!" His voice resounded through the church, followed by shouts of Amen from the congregation. "This is your invitation," he continued. "Let us all stand. And while you are standing, if you need more light in your life, you need to come. Come up and cry out to the Lord."

I cannot explain what had compelled me from my seat then, but an immense weight had lifted from my shoulders as I walked to the front of the congregation and stood before the minister. Tears had streamed down my face, and yet I'd felt a tremendous joy. Somehow, I knew I was doing the right thing. I did not yet comprehend the light that the minister spoke of, but I wanted it.

Just as the minister's words had spoken to something deep in my soul on that day, it seemed Brandt's grandmother had spoken to his soul and touched upon a sense of moral duty in Brandt. Perhaps in that moment, he felt God had charged him with the salvation of Amber Guyger's soul. That must have been it, for nothing else could explain what I witnessed next.

Slowly, perhaps even hesitantly, Brandt made his way from the bench to the witness stand. As I sat watching him, I became acutely aware of my surroundings: the police officers in the room, my brother's body walking in their midst, the walls that enclosed us in this place, and the brick reinforcing them on the outside. One of the officers shifted his weight from one foot to the other while another seemed to tense as Brandt entered the aisle that led to the front of the room.

I looked ahead of Brandt to the witness stand. I had sat there twice during the trial. During the testimony, I spoke about my last moments with Botham. At the penalty phase, after the verdict but before the impact statement, I spoke to the effect Botham's death had on me and my family. Both times, the witness stand had seemed harmless enough. But now, it looked like a prison.

The table and all of the benches between me and where Brandt would sit were like an impenetrable fortress. He suddenly seemed so far away from me and so close to law enforcement. Even the judge, who had a minister's smile on her face, one that was at once placid and satisfied to see that a member of the congregation had been moved to action, suddenly looked every bit like a jailer. Or an executioner. Once Brandt sat behind that table, I began plotting the quickest paths to him. I did not know what he would do or what he would say, but I knew I had to be able to get to him if I needed to. I had been too far away to do that for Botham, but Brandt was right before my eyes.

Brandt paused for a second, his hands flat on the table as if to steady the entire earth, his mouth slightly open as if words were already coming from his mouth, his eyes fixed on the back of the room.

"I . . ." he said, pausing briefly to look at Guyger before returning his gaze to the back of the room. "I don't want to say twice or for the hundredth time how much you've taken from us. I think you know that."

If only I had the ability to fly, I thought as he spoke. *I could fly over these benches to him in an instant. Faster than anyone else could get to him, faster than a speeding—*

"But I just . . ." His words trailed off as he lowered his head and exhaled with what seemed to be the weight of not having spoken his mind through the entire trial. I could hear the pain in his silence, and I wanted to go up there and carry him away from all of this. And still, I was curious.

If he does not wish to tell her what she has taken from us, what could he possibly wish to tell her?

He shifted uneasily in his seat and continued. "I hope you go to God with all the guilt, all the bad things you may have done in the past. Each and every one of us may have done something we were not supposed to do."

Yes, we may have. But how many of us have taken a life?

"If you truly are sorry, I know . . ." His words faded again and seemed to change his thought. "I speak for myself. I forgive you."

When he spoke those words, I felt the entire room fall away, and all that remained was a black void into which a spotlight shined on him, Guyger, and me. Words continued to come from his mouth, and I looked on in stunned silence. It seemed that even Brandt did not know which words would come out of his mouth; he had not planned them. Still, I could not believe *these* words.

"If you go to God and ask Him, He will forgive you."

I felt ill. I knew he was right. We are all taught the same thing, that God forgives all sins—the small ones and the big ones alike.

But forgiveness is not the same as justice, I hoped. *Not on earth and not in heaven. That's why there is a hell.*

Brandt tugged at his collar as if the next words were so heavy they would not form nor rise from his throat if he did not make room for them.

"And I don't think anyone can say . . ." he paused again, for the words were indeed heavy, and his soul labored to bring them forth into the world. "I speak for myself, not even for my family. But I love you just like I love everyone else."

My entire body grew numb, and though I heard his next words, my mind became fixed on just one.

Love.

"And I'm not gonna say I hope you rot and die."

Love. A murderer. Like they're everyone else.

". . . just like my brother did . . ."

I was not even sure I was judging his words in that moment, only processing them. They were English—they must have been English because that is the only language we speak. But it was like I was hearing a foreign language I had studied for years but never spoken. I could hear the words, but I could not make sense of them.

How can he speak of love toward his brother's killer? And to love her like he loves everyone else? Did he love her like he loved Botham?

Brandt loosened his collar again.

He is hot. Or he is forcing himself to say these words. God, I hope it is the latter.

As the reality of his words settled in, the room took shape around us once again. And then I noticed the benches and the table between Brandt and me, not because I sought to carry him away from any danger I perceived from the room, but because I wished to stop his words. Somehow, I felt he said them against his will. His silence seemed louder because the microphone picked up every swallow he made during his pauses.

"I wasn't going to ever say this in front of my family or anyone, but . . ."

Then don't say it. Don't say anything more. Don't!

"I don't even want you to go to jail." His voice nearly caught in his throat as he said these last words, and I felt an even stronger desire to rescue him from the torment of these words, to stop him saying them, and to stop me from hearing them.

"Because I know that's exactly what Botham would want you to do," he said, and I knew that these were not his words any longer. Perhaps they never were. He was appealing to her soul. He was the minister, and he was conducting his own benediction.

Turning the witness stand into his pulpit and altar, he continued. "I want the best for you, and the best would be to give your life to Christ. I think giving your life to Christ would be the best thing that Botham would want you to do. Again, I love you as a person. I don't wish anything bad on you."

His voice cracked then, and he reached under his glasses to wipe a tear from his eye. His call to the altar was complete. Now, all Guyger had to do was make up her mind and answer the call. Only, Brandt was not going to give her a choice.

"I don't know if this is possible," he began, a tremor still present in his voice, "but can I give her a hug? Please?" There was silence as he looked at the judge and the judge looked to the defense team. "Please?" Brandt implored once more before bodies began stirring in the room. I looked at the law officers, who seemed even more tense. Then I looked to the judge, who had taken a handkerchief and had begun dabbing at her moist eyes. I was bewildered. I may as well have been in a dream.

"Yes," the judge answered, still wiping her eyes. Then Brandt stood, and it was as if there was never a barrier between him and Guyger, so quickly did it seem that he went from sitting to standing before the judge with that woman in his arms.

My desire to get up from my seat and leap over the benches to Brandt, who now held our brother's killer in his arms, was palpable. My body was hot all over, my legs were like wound coils, and my hands made fists. But I did not move. I could only watch as the two embraced for what felt like an eternity.

Chapter Twelve

I did not cry when my father died. I hardly knew the man. And I did not admire him. He impregnated my mother when she was fourteen, too young to have children. That was the only thing he contributed to my life.

Some people hoped that his death might have provided some closure for me, or that its untimeliness robbed me of much-needed closure. Truthfully speaking, though, I needed no such closure. Perhaps there is something tragic to the fact that I will never mourn a father the way that a child ought to when he is gone. Still, I knew that it is the child who mourns the father, not the other way around. Bertrum Jean was not supposed to bury his son. So I will never forget the testimony he gave just before Guyger's sentencing and Brandt's impact statement.

"J-E-A-N," he had said, pronouncing the spelling of his name with a certain flair and confidence that belied the heavy heart with which he took the stand. Above his brow were creases that hinted subtly at his age and perhaps even the worry that Botham's death had brought him, but the creases around his mouth could only have been made by a lifetime of smiling. Botham had already been getting similar creases, though he was still a few years from his thirtieth birthday. As I watched Bertrum testify about the memories he would always have of his son, I thought those creases nearly made him look as though he was smiling. And the joy that Botham had brought him, the joy that had been permanently etched into Bertrum's face, made his sorrow all the more palpable.

"You are the father of Botham Jean," the attorney asked him. To this he hesitated ever so briefly.

How ought he respond to such a question? In the present tense? Or the past?

"Yes, I am," he replied before giving an account of raising Botham as a working man while my mother attended university.

As he spoke, I remembered Botham as a joyful baby. I would go away to live in the United States while he was still a child, but we were close whether I was near or far. I was there when he grew adamant about being baptized and singing in our church choir. It seemed that Botham had always been the same person, even as a child. As I watched his father break down on the witness stand, it occurred to me that none of us would get over his death, but Bertrum most certainly would not.

And why should he? When a loved one dies from a disease, the disease goes with him. We understand the nature of diseases. As tragic as they are, they are purposed with taking lives. Police officers should not be. If a person dies of cancer, the cancer goes with them. But the person who took Botham's life will go on living free in a few short years.

"You said that you can no longer look forward to Sundays?" the attorney asked Bertrum. At this question, he broke down again. I immediately understood his tears were not simply for the tragic past but also for the imminent future.

How can we ever get over Botham's death? Every moment of our lives was envisioned with Botham in it. We are doomed to live always looking ahead to that future and wondering how it would have been with Botham in it. Because he was supposed to be there.

As I listened to Bertrum sob, I considered the futility of life. Even my anger felt powerless in the wake of this thought.

How can I look forward to anything again? I wondered. *But even more important, what reason do I have to fight for—well, anything?* The trial had given me some sense of purpose. I had to be sure that Botham received justice. But by the end of the trial, I realized that the guilty verdict was not enough. I then felt powerless to achieve anything else. Furthermore, I felt hopeless that my own condition would change. There was nothing to stop the shaking in my body or fill the emptiness in my soul.

We spent ten days in that courthouse. Ten days of attorneys and police officers and detectives hoping to deny that a crime had been committed against Botham. Ten days of inconsolable tears. Ten days of reliving his murder and being reminded that I will never see him again made me numb. Long after my mother and Bertrum had given their penalty phase testimonies, long after the judge had handed down the ten-year sentence to Guyger, and long after Brandt had forgiven and hugged Guyger during the witness impact statements, I remained on the bench. Much of my family had stood and gone, but I could not stand. I know that my aunt stayed by my side, but I could not feel her touch. I did not want to accept the sentence.

There must be something left to say. Some motion to pass. A forgotten testimony. Our statements must not have been understood; otherwise, our tears were in vain. How can everyone be leaving the courtroom now?

Before long, Bertrum was also by my side, beckoning me to stand and leave the room. But I shrugged him off. Leaving meant conceding that sentencing.

Stop being so eager to concede things, I would have shouted to my family if I could have mustered the strength to do anything other than sob into a handkerchief.

Get back here and fight for Botham with me!

But the fighting was all done. I'd had to accept that Botham was dead in order to even walk into this courthouse. To walk out of it, I would have to accept that we had done all we could to get him justice.

Simply standing seemed impossible to me, so I could not fathom the ease with which everyone had exited the courtroom. Bertrum had to put his arms around me and guide me so that I could follow the judge's order to clear the room. But all I could think in that moment was that he reminded me so much of Botham. As he held me and led me from the courtroom, I again imagined it was Botham who led me. This was only a fleeting thought though. Botham was gone, and the justice system had done all it was going to do.

When I finally stood up and left the courtroom, the sun was shining brightly into the glass hall, but my world darkened as I got closer and closer to the building's exit. Outside, I stood beside my mother as she gave a rousing speech about the change that needed to be brought to Dallas in the wake of our tragedy.

I did not say much to anyone, not even to Brandt, whose decision, although perplexing, was between him and God. I felt I had no right to interfere with or question the way in which he chose to grieve for or honor his big brother. I did not feel that was anyone's right, not even his own flesh and blood. And yet there were complete strangers who felt not only the need but the moral justification and self-righteousness to trash him for a decision that was his alone to make, a decision that most of them had never faced and could not fathom making. According to them, because of Brandt's decision, we were no longer worthy of sympathy. In Brandt's moment of grief, in his hope to find closure for his dead brother and perhaps honor him in a most heavy and significant moment, it seemed that everyone outside of that room thought he should be thinking about them and their opinions about some movement, whether he knew what they were or not, whether those opinions were varied or represented some monolith or not. It seemed they wanted to cancel him for not thinking of them but for thinking about how best to handle his *own* inner turmoil. He made a choice in his own soul, and they found a way to be offended, they who did not know him and most of whom had probably never thought about him until they had a moment to judge him.

I listened to media personalities and commenters say what they could have or would have done. Then they made Brandt responsible for their emotions; they burdened him with upholding some unwritten principle of their movement, as if the burden of losing his brother hadn't been a big enough burden for an eighteen-year-old. All he wanted was to heal. And all they could do was pile on to his burden, make it heavier for him. I know because I felt that heaviness.

Even if I did not share his sentiment, even if I could find no place in my heart at all to forgive Amber Guyger the way he could, I am his big sister. His pain was mine.

Allies are not allies if they cannot put themselves in the shoes of those for whom they claim to advocate. Imagine seeing someone experience a tragedy and then telling them, "You have my sympathy, but only as long as you grieve the way I want you to do it." How monstrous to be outraged by the manner of someone else's grief! That is what Brandt and our family had to deal with in the aftermath of his forgiving Amber Guyger.

We were no longer simply grieving. Suddenly, because of Brandt's actions, we were spitting in the faces of the entire Black Lives Matter movement. According to Charlamagne Tha God, we were also perpetuating some tragic flaw in the Black community that makes us forgive White folks but not our own folks. Suddenly, we were not thankful for the support of Black people. Why couldn't we—and most of all, why couldn't Brandt—simply be grieving? In that moment, it seemed my family and I somehow became offenders in our own tragedy.

The vitriol we faced only worsened my pain. My brother had been murdered. Yet I had just faced a justice system hell-bent on turning a murderer into a victim. My brother was dead. Yet I was hearing the chatter of people who thought I owed them something in the wake of my loss, self-appointed gatekeepers who were ready to declare that my brother's death at the hands of a White police officer did not count if we grieved differently. It seemed that Botham's life did not matter to anyone who could not benefit from his death. In the face of that reality, my anger began to morph into a deep depression.

Chapter Thirteen

We started the Botham Jean Foundation just a few months after his death. We hosted our first red-tie gala, a celebration of Botham's life and legacy, in the middle of the trial on what would have been Botham's twenty-eighth birthday. It was a bittersweet moment.

Celebrating Botham's birthday without him was always difficult. And the pressures of the trial were daunting. But it was also important to host the gala as a testament for what Botham stood for. He was a faithful member of the Church of Christ. He was an advocate for community outreach in Saint Lucia. And he was a man passionate about missionary work. On a day when many people were simply wondering what would happen to Botham's killer, and on a day when the world seemed so dark for my family and me, it was necessary to have a moment of light.

The gala was a splendid affair. Every man wore a red tie, and every woman wore a dress in Botham's favorite shade of red. Artists painted portraits depicting Botham's luminous smile. A violinist gave the party a jazzy vibe. Spoken-word artists recited poems dedicated to Botham's memory. A woman with a powerful voice sang a Christian song whose defining line was "He has done enough." Of course, its subject was God and His blessings, but it also seemed to fit the theme that although Botham's life had been cut short, he had done enough in that time to leave a resounding impact on the communities he touched.

For the briefest of moments, the world felt benevolent. I was grateful for every one of the people who showed up and celebrated Botham, although I was wary of those who might only be there to advance their own agendas. I wanted to believe that everyone was there for Botham, but the way in which the whole day began made believing hard to do.

It was difficult to plan a celebration of Botham's life in the middle of a trial that had yet to determine the outcome of his murder. The politicians in Dallas did not make that planning any easier. A few even suggested I move the red-tie gala to a day other than Botham's birthday because the date coincided with an important Dallas Cowboys football game. I held steadfast to the stance that anyone who considered a football game more important than Botham's life ought to skip our gala.

Perhaps the most egregious act happened on the morning of the gala. My family and I were in Dallas for the event; therefore we spent the morning at the Dallas West Church of Christ, the church Botham had regularly attended.

The congregation had just finished raising their voices melodically to the ceiling of the sanctuary. I had often found myself staring at that wooden octagon up there, wishing that I could see past it and get some glimpse of heaven. Just to know it was there. It was while I was searching for that glimpse that I heard Botham's name spoken into the microphone. I looked up to see the Mayor of Dallas, Eric Johnson, speaking with a commanding voice.

"It's always good to come home," Mayor Johnson said. "Dallas West may not be my church home anymore, but it will always *be* home. And I will always return to it."

Murmurs of affirmation rose among the congregation, and the nodding heads were like a ripple through the pews. I remained unaffected: no Amen stirred in my throat, and my head was still as I gazed at the mayor. I wanted him to look at me. I tried to will him to look me in my eyes as he spoke. But although his gaze perused the entire room, it never seemed to find me.

"But today isn't about me," Mayor Johnson continued. "It's about Botham." Whispers of "yes" and "Amen" grew louder among the congregation. Even my mother nodded her head beside me. I wondered if the mayor saw her.

"He would have been twenty-eight years old today," Mayor Johnson said. "And even if the Lord saw fit to call him home—to his true home early—we know that this place will always be his home."

"Amen!" The voice came from someone seated to my left. But when I looked to see who it was, I could not look past the tears streaming down Brandt's face.

"I just want to express my condolences to the family," Mayor Johnson continued. "And if they have a little time after the service today, I would love to speak with them."

I looked at him again, but he was already walking away from the microphone, his eyes fixed on the seat toward which he was heading.

After the service, my family and I waited in one of the meeting rooms for several minutes. I heard his voice just outside the door, but it faded away as one of his representatives entered the room instead. The man, clean-shaven from crown to chin, walked over to me and spoke quietly.

"Mayor Johnson is requesting that only immediate family be in attendance," the representative said. He seemed to want only me to hear the request and carry it out, but my mother heard some of his words and approached.

"We are all family here," Allison said in a firm tone, to which the representative replied more audibly for everyone to hear.

"Yes, I understand that you're all family, but the mayor was only hoping to speak with Botham's immediate family."

"Why is that?" I asked indignantly. "Why does it matter which family members hear?"

"I didn't ask him," the representative replied. "I only know that he won't come in until only the parents and siblings are in attendance."

"That is fine," Aunt Desma said calmly. "We can wait outside." She then departed with several uncles and cousins, and after a while Mayor Johnson entered the room. His lips were parted in what seemed to me to be a rehearsed smile, but it quickly faded when he noticed that one of our attorneys, Daryl Washington, was still in attendance. He frowned.

"I thought I said immediate family only." His voice lacked the sympathy it had in his earlier speech to the congregation.

"He is like our family," Allison Jean said. "Anything you have to say to us, you can say to him." The mayor swallowed hard and clenched his jaw. Then he stormed out of the room. It was apparent to me that Mayor Johnson had no intention of speaking before anyone he considered a rival. And that is how he viewed everyone on our legal team; they were a team made up of none of his lawyers. At the outset of our trial, Mayor Eric Johnson petitioned us heavily with the hopes that we would choose his law firm. We did not. Perhaps he still thought there was a chance we would change our minds. There was not.

I do not know what the mayor had intended to say to us at Botham's church. When my family and I left the building, I noticed him fuming in his car. Perhaps he had meant to be gone by the time we left, but he had evidently forgotten something. He had to look through us as he waited for his children to exit the doors behind us.

The moment for Botham's first red-tie gala was most certainly marred by the trial, and I sometimes felt that I had to overcome the very people whom I looked to for help. I understand that life was going on for everyone else, but it would have been nice not to have had my family tragedy considered in the same breath as a Sunday night football game. And whatever Mayor Johnson's and my differences may be, I was greatly pained to feel that one of the most powerful Black men in Dallas had come to my brother's church on his birthday, not looking to lend me a hand but instead looking to further some agenda of his that I may never know. Nevertheless, the commemorative gala was a much-needed blessing in a tumultuous time for me and my family.

In the aftermath of Guyger's verdict and sentencing, the Botham Jean Foundation immediately went to work with the charitable institutions of Saint Lucia as well as with any cause that would continue to seek justice for Botham.

In June of 2021, we worked with Representative Carl Sherman and Texas Governor Greg Abbott to pass the Botham Jean Act, also known as "Bo's Law." Under this new law, police officers are prohibited from turning off their body cams or dash cams during a traffic stop or arrest. That this was not a law before meant that police officers used (or rather, didn't use) the cameras to their advantage to provide as little evidence as possible for Botham's investigation. The very institution tasked with finding justice for Botham was hell-bent on minimizing the very tools that would help them find that justice. Now there was a law named after their victim that would, hopefully, inhibit their ability to victimize anyone else.

Chapter Fourteen

At the beginning of 2022, I felt I had reached the peak of my depression. When a person reaches such a peak, they are as low as they can go. But it doesn't feel like you're in a hole. It feels like being at the top of a building, toeing a ledge. So as I watched the news on the morning of January 30, I felt like I could have been Chelsie Kryst. I could have stood where she stood. I could have felt that wind on my face.

"Mom, do you want tea?" I heard Jareem ask me from my bedroom doorway. "I can make you some." At first, I did not reply. All of my attention was on the news report, on the yellow tape, on the red lights that flashed across my television screen.

"No," I said, my eyes still glued to the television. "Go downstairs. I'll be down in a minute."

"Mom?" he made one more attempt to get my attention. Perhaps he knew I was retreating inside myself. Maybe he was trying to pull me back. But I could no longer hear him.

"Mom . . ." His voice faded into the background of the reporter's voice.

"This is a woman who showed so much promise," she said. "But last night, she decided to end it all."

I looked at a place behind the yellow tape where she must have landed, and I felt a strange emotion: envy. I wished that I were her. Not for all of her beauty and accomplishments, but because she had escaped the pain.

I remembered she had once mentioned that she felt blindsided by the online hate she experienced for being so "old" when she won Miss America, for embracing her race, for being too muscular to be beautiful. Society used her vulnerabilities to bring her pain. Why? Because they felt good ridiculing her age and ignoring how little they had accomplished at their much older ages; because it was easier to hate her muscles and not their own fat; because they felt virtuous when they ignored her race, not ignorant of a not-so-distant past when she would have been kept from competing. They built themselves up on her pain, and I felt that I knew something about that pain. Throughout my journey to seek justice for Botham's murder, it seemed that I could only find people who wanted to raise themselves—on his coffin if necessary. So I could not help imagining what it might have been like for her in her last moments.

The air is so cold on my face that it is becoming numb. I wonder if I will even feel it when I hit the icy pavement below. I think it will be like hitting an off switch. I have been on my whole life. And for what? What is the purpose of all this when someone can just take it away? They can take it away and no one will be held responsible. I can be on my whole life. And I can be so good. I can be a track star and Miss America and a television personality. I can be a model student and the best accountant, a natural-born leader and a model Christian. And then someone can take your life just like that. Where is the reason in that? What was the purpose of your faith then? How powerful—

"Mom!" my eldest yelled from the kitchen. "I made you tea."

"I'm on my way down now," I said, but not loud enough for anyone to hear. My eyes were glued to the television. A model had died in New York early that morning. It was a suicide. She had decided she'd had enough. Enough being beautiful. Enough being famous. Enough being.

Enough simply being.

I tried to imagine her body over the shoulder of the reporter and past the parked police cars. For a moment, I wished that I could have talked to her. To know what had brought her down. There must have been something so terrible to burden her. And it outweighed all of the good in her life. I was the opposite. I had lots of good things in my life. But the bigness of Botham's goodness . . . Gosh, it was so massive. And his absence was gargantuan. Like a black hole. Crushing me. I turned the television off, but I remained staring at its empty screen and again longed to be that model.

Some people think that the opposite of anger is happiness. But I know this to be untrue. Joy and anger are, in fact, similar in so many ways, the least of which is that they are both catalysts to action. Maybe anger is a little different because it can be wildly destructive and reactive, but it is still an active emotion. When people are angry, they are moved to action. They throw things. They fight. The speak out, yelling and screaming. Anger is not always productive, but it moves the world one way or another. Entire kingdoms have risen and fallen over anger. Revolutions have been fought. Paintings scrawled. Books written. Joy does a few of these things and is the result of some of the others. No, joy is not the opposite of anger. Sadness is. Melancholy. Depression.

The thing about depression is that it is a paralytic. It stops action in its tracks. Depression, then, can be far more seductive than either joy or anger because it requires nothing on your part. No thing. No thought. No movement. You do not even have to make the effort to not do something. If I become too happy, I may have to restrain myself to make others comfortable. If I become too angry, I have to work hard not to slap somebody in the face. But depression doesn't require you to resist the urge to stay in bed. You simply don't get out. And I didn't.

On those first days after the trial, I didn't know that I had entered a depression. I only knew that I would often lie so very still in my bed long after waking. I did not even wish to move. I opened my eyes because that is an involuntary action, like breathing or my heart beating. But I did not move a muscle that lay beneath my quilts and sheets.

Doesn't this feel good? Now go back to sleep. Forever.

Melancholy is not laziness either. Even laziness has a little feeling of guilt in it, a feeling that you ought to be doing something.

Sometimes, you would love to go that party. There is an impetus to get dressed, look good, and be seen even though doing none of these things would be far easier. There is an impetus toward being productive, toward achieving a goal. I felt no such impetus, and I had no guilt for not feeling it. Perhaps I shook off my melancholy long enough to go to church or work, or to take the children to school. But when the pandemic shut down the world, I not only lost the desire to leave the house, I no longer had to.

On the day I saw the news of that model's suicide, I wished we were still in the lockdown phase of the pandemic. It would have made it easier to remain in my bed all day. Still as a corpse.

Chapter Fifteen

In June of 2020, eight months after the trial, my family was one of eight families who met with President Trump under the assumption that he would help us make progress on police reform. It was an unremarkably cloudy day in Washington D.C., and it would ultimately yield an unremarkable result. I would say the same for most of the politicians I met.

Perhaps under any other circumstances, I may have walked into the White House and looked at every person there with awe. But given the weight of the problem—the problem the eight families faced and, indeed, the problem the nation faced, as well as my desire to find solutions—it was hard not to look at these politicians and simply see them as regular people stepping on each other's toes to achieve absolutely nothing.

President Trump could have been any other old man with uncouth hair sitting before me in that room. It was not difficult to tell him that I did not want my picture taken with him and that the meeting we all were to have needed to be closed-door. I know not from where I got the strength to speak to anyone, especially a president, so matter-of-factly. I like to think Botham gave me the strength to fight for justice. Before his death, I was not always the most vocal. I did not always speak up. Even against a church that did not allow women a voice, I did as I was told. And I did not have the voice to match my outrage when I saw Black men and women shot down by police prior to 2018.

The pandemic, in this regard, was a pivotal moment for me. My outrage had always been there, but Botham gave me the strength to fight. When George Floyd died at the hands of police officers in Minnesota, that is when I found my voice to fight. When President Trump agreed to see the families of the slain to discuss police reform, I was ready for that fight.

Even as he ambled toward me, as most seventy-four-year-olds are given to do, the words poured freely from my mouth.

"I don't want a picture taken," I said. "We're not here for that. If you're serious about police reform, we don't need the theatrics of it." A few members of the families in attendance tried to veil their disappointment. Some of the more politically inclined, whether they were actual politicians or just aspiring ones, wore their disappointment on their sleeves. Nevertheless, we had the meeting behind closed doors, and it seemed, at the beginning of the whole ordeal, that our concerns would be taken seriously.

My first hint that things would not go our way should have been the large number of police officers in attendance. I, along with the families of Trayvon Martin, Ahmaud Arbery, and Eric Garner, met with the president in a large room, and on all sides of us were armed sheriffs. Certainly, they were there as part of the conversation, but they may as well have been human bars in a cage the way they were present and in full uniform. Deer could not have been made more uncomfortable if they had been forced to graze in a field surrounded by lions.

"To each of you," the president began, "I want you to know that all Americans grieve with you."

All of them? I wondered. *Somehow, I doubt that.*

He continued, "Their deaths will not have been for nothing. Let us see what we can do, how we can work together on this."

Looking around, I could see that a few members of the families were moved by what seemed to them to be genuine concern on the part of the president.

"I cannot imagine the depth of your pain," he said, "but I can promise you that I will continue to fight hard for our people."

Our people? Is it so hard to say Black people?

It was hard to listen to him while sitting among so many armed officers. I was reminded of the many police officers who were brought in to surround the courtroom during Botham's trial—and to protect Guyger in the event that she would be attacked during the verdict and sentencing. I had agreed to the meeting because I was determined to effect change, whether I found that opportunity with Democrats or Republicans. However, when he gave his speech to the cameras afterward, President Trump's words slowly wore away at the hope that anything meaningful would be done as a result of our meeting.

"Law and order must be restored," he declared before the podium. "The looters have no cause that they're fighting for—just trouble."

Will you say anything about the protesters?

"Americans know the truth," he continued. "Without police, there is chaos."

Is that even up for debate right now? What does that have to do with police officers who are killing Black people?

He then signed an executive order to raise the standard of police practices. But that hardly addressed the issue. He got his photo op—his moment to grin before the camera with a meaningless piece of paper and say that he had accomplished something. Yet he also made it clear that any meaningful law would be up to Congress. If he had signed that executive order the same day he was sworn into office, Botham would still be dead today.

Although I went to Washington D.C. with an unfathomable strength to fight, my experience there diminished that strength somewhat. And I knew that I would go home with no significant accomplishment. Just the memory of a piece of paper. And a former reality TV star's signature scribbled on it.

Chapter Sixteen

I take one step over the edge and feel my body become weightless. My other foot follows inadvertently. Before long, my whole body is falling though the New York morning air. I certainly feel the wind in my face and over my whole body. No, I did not attend law school. But I wish I had. Perhaps that would have made my conversation with the senator from South Carolina easier.

"Look," he began, "I know I invited you up here for a discussion. You should know that the issue of qualified immunity is a dead issue."

I struggled to find meaning in his words. They did not match his actions of just moments before: his welcoming smile, his seeming openness to having a discussion. Even meeting in his office had been his idea. But now that I was here, I was having a hard time making sense of the words that were coming out of his mouth. Maybe I was just too distracted.

"So why did you invite me up here?" I asked.

"I wanted the chance to explain the matter to you face-to-face," he said. "Away from the crowd. I worked very hard to bring this bill to Congress. But a few of the things Democrats want are just dead issues."

The man in front of me had dark skin, but I could see where his hairline had remained and where it had long ago left him. There were so many corners and divots in his head too. What looked to be a scar, the ghost of what must have been a very bloody incident, was carved right into the middle of his forehead. It, along with his very thin eyebrows, gave his face a look of perpetual worry. Or surprise.

"It's a matter of money," he continued.

"What about money?" I replied.

"The insurance premiums for the police departments would be through the roof."

"Isn't that all taxpayer dollars anyway?"

"It's a more complicated situation that."

"Is it?"

"It always is."

His face was so round. Like a clementine. A bit too wide and not quite long enough. It made his cleft chin look completely out of place. Like God was just looking for another place to put a dimple. As if He knew that the man before me would grow up to have a pudgy face and a jawline that completely disappeared into his neck.

"Listen," he continued. "I have tried my best to make this a bipartisan bill. I mean, we all want the same thing. Even the senator from New Jersey knows that I have been as earnest as I could be."

I did not doubt his earnestness. I believe he wanted to get something done, or at least look like he was trying to get something done. That was why I was in this office that was somehow even smaller than I imagined it would be.

"And you know," he went on, "I had the guts to reject President Trump's executive order. I did that." He thumped his index finger emphatically on his sprawling desk. "And do you know why?"

I realized he wanted me to ask him a question. It did not matter that he had already asked the question himself. As long as I said something and then he said something, then we were having a discussion. Texas Ranger David Armstrong had done something similar when he had "met with Botham's family." He could literally provide no answers to our questions. But he did meet with us. A familiar but fleeting phrase came to the tip of my tongue— something about skinfolk and kinfolk.

"Why?" I asked.

"Because it wouldn't do enough," he answered with a proud grin and gums that were bigger than his teeth. "Because I knew that this was an issue that needed to be handled at the state and local levels. You know, people who know what things look like on the ground."

"People who could decide just how accountable an officer should be when he shoots someone?" I added.

"Exactly," the senator replied. I wanted to sigh or roll my eyes, but he might think I was gasping with excitement or that I had something in my eye.

"Look," he said as I began to notice how often he appealed to one of the five senses before he started a ramble. "No one is more disappointed than I am that this did not pass. Democrats have once again squandered a critical chance to implement meaningful reform to make our neighborhoods less dangerous and mend the tenuous relationships between law enforcement and communities of color."

He used so many syllables. There was no way he had not written that down and rehearsed it before he'd said it to me. But one thing he said did stand out.

"How meaningful can the reform be if qualified immunity is off the table?" I asked.

"Listen," he said, "no Republican is going anywhere near that. They're just not."

"Then why did you invite me in here?" I asked.

"Because I did not want you to think that I was deliberately ignoring you," the senator replied.

"And yet, you are ignoring me, aren't you?"

"If I could do more, I would."

"Would you?"

"Let me be clear: the people who are leaving the table are the Democrats. The senator from New Jersey and I have had some very good conversations."

I did not want to hear about their "good conversations." I wanted to know why qualified immunity was a dead issue. Maybe I wanted to debate the merits or at least just learn more. It being a dead issue meant that this conversation was a dead one.

My gaze moved on from his face to the contents of the office. There was a flag on either side of him, an American one on the left and a South Carolinian one on the right. There were bookshelves along one entire wall, and each was filled with books, thick volumes that were crammed in so that you could read their spines, and several others that lay on top of the shelves or were open to one page or another. It all looked so busy. Even his desk had papers and open volumes at its fringes.

The office was a claustrophobic square of a room, but the person who occupied it was supposed to be tasked with the biggest ideas, purposed with actions that change the world. And yet, when I looked at the man across from me, I saw a man who had spent an entire year on a bill, only to get as far as I had gotten. The only difference is that I had done nothing yet. What was to stop me from trying to do more than what he had done? Why should I be sitting here wishing he would do something and then worrying that he hadn't. He was a human being. Just like me.

"Why?" I blurted out, interrupting whatever long-winded explanation he was giving to a question he had probably posed himself. He looked at me, a bit stunned.

"Why what?" he asked.

"Why is qualified immunity a dead issue?" I asked. He sighed, and deep creases spread across his wide forehead.

"Look—" he began.

"No," I interrupted. "I don't want to look. Just tell me."

"The bottom line is every politician, whether you're talking about a senator or even a president, has a core constituency. Mine, and for that matter all Republicans, have a core that includes law enforcement. We conservatives, as a matter of moral hazard, are very supportive of law enforcement."

"So it is not a matter of what is right but a matter of what you hope your voters will do in the next election?"

"Well, that is part of it. Here's the other part: law enforcement will never be in favor of a situation in which individual officers are being made to worry about how . . ." He trailed off, realizing he was about to reveal something he shouldn't. "Well, more civil responsibilities."

"You mean they don't want to be held accountable for mistakes that they make," I remarked.

"I think that is a simplistic way of putting it," he replied.

"But it's not wrong."

"In a manner of speaking." He paused to gather his thoughts. "I'll say this. If you put police officers under the kind of scrutiny they would be required to be under without qualified immunity, you're going to get far fewer of them policing those more challenging communities."

"And what makes those areas so challenging to begin with?"

"Well, that is a more complex question with, I'm sure, a more complex answer."

"Is it?" I asked.

"It always is."

With this comment, I stood to leave. I shook his hand because he offered it. But it was hard not to shout at him about how useless he was. As I continued down the long hall, I could not shake the feeling that every effort I made to be at the White House and in front of those many consider to be the most powerful people in the world was a most futile ordeal. I was not sure I'd accomplished anything, and I could have done that from my bed.

Chapter Seventeen

I think that I was jealous of her, jealous of her suicide. Every day since her tragedy, and every day that I woke up to face a day without Botham, I envied the former Miss America's feet on her balcony, each step she took one after another until she found her toes just over the edge. I could have been her. I felt her pain. And I wished I could feel her freedom.

Cheslie Kryst was a model, an attorney, a beauty pageant titleholder, and a television correspondent. But our pretty isn't always pretty enough. Our intelligence isn't always intelligent enough. Our safe isn't always safe enough. Even among my own people, it seemed that my injustice wasn't unjust enough. Not unless it could benefit someone else. I learned that lesson when I got a call from a woman who went by the name of Queen and who considered herself the head of the self-proclaimed "Botham Jean Memorial Council."

"Well, I think we can help," the woman on the other end of the phone said.

"Go on," I replied.

"We can make it so that the very street that those police officers have to go to every day is named after Botham Jean," she explained. "Having the street named after him should be a daily reminder to everyone who works in that precinct, anyone who was responsible for training the officer who killed your brother, and those responsible for trying to cover it up."

"Yes," I replied. "Yes to all of that. What would be the first steps?"

"Well, we should meet up first to go over the logistics," she said. "Are you still in Dallas?"

"I am."

"Good. Let's meet for coffee. I know a good spot, and I can bring along a good friend of mine, Adam. He was actually responsible for starting the petition to get the street name changed."

"Sure," I said. "Text me when and where, and I will be there."

I ended the call and sighed with an exasperation that was beginning to seep into my bones. I had been receiving so many calls about Botham. Condolences had become a distant memory, so most of these calls were from people who needed Botham's name to suit themselves. They needed permission to make a documentary, or they wanted to tie my family's name and support to their project without ever meeting us or having our support.

For Queen and Adam, this meant starting an organization named after my brother. They could have used any name. Perhaps they should have if their goal was truly to honor slain Black men. But they needed recognition, and Botham had about as high-profile a name as one could have in Dallas. Furthermore, once they had already formed their Botham Jean Memorial Council, they needed me. After all, how could an organization named after Botham Jean be earnest without one of his family members being a part of it? And if they were earnest about honoring Botham, I wanted to meet them. Of course, if they weren't so earnest, I still wanted to meet them; there is a saying about where one should keep both, one's friends and one's enemies. So a few weeks after I received their call, I was eager to head back down to Dallas.

February of 2020 was approximately four months after Botham's trial, and I was committed to keeping his memory and his name alive. Our civil trial against the Dallas Police Department did not seem to be going anywhere, and that same police department seemed both pleased and determined to put us out of their memory. Getting the street where the police department was located named after Botham would ensure that they would never forget. It was the right move. I just wanted to be sure it was also being done by the right people and for the right reasons.

I landed in Dallas on a cool February day and arrived at the coffee shop on time—about fifteen minutes before Queen and Adam showed up. I had just enough time to breathe—to truly focus on breathing. The trial was only a few months behind me, but it still felt like it was just yesterday. The aftermath of the trial made every holiday an absolute blur in my mind. Thanksgiving, Christmas, and New Year's, all came and went. I did not celebrate any of them. Neither Thanksgiving nor Christmas would ever be the same without Botham. New Year's Day was just a reminder of another year that he would not get to live. Valentine's Day had been a few days ago. I didn't care.

When Queen and Adam walked through the door, they were fully in character. Queen wore a headwrap and daishiki, and Adam was dressed similarly, but his locks flowed all the way down his back.

"Hello, queen!" Queen announced when she saw me.

"Nice to meet you . . . um, Queen?" I said hesitantly.

"Yeah, that's my name," she said. "But I call every woman that— every *Black* woman. You know, cuz we're all queens, right?"

"Sure," I said.

"You know Adam," she continued, indicating her friend with the long locks.

"You mentioned him," I said.

"My sistah!" he said, sticking out his hand. I took it and he dragged me into a hug.

"Oh!" I said, taken aback.

A bit too familiar, I thought.

"Yes," Queen said, clearly approving of our meeting. "He's the gentleman who started the petition. He's a friend of mine. We go to the same church; he's been at these protests with me."

"Okay," I said.

"So we were working on the street name change," Queen continued, "but we're kind of at an impasse because of the difficulty getting the people who live on that street to sign."

"And you know the police department ain't trying to help," Adam chimed in.

"But we're working on it," Queen reiterated. "When we got that together, I was coming for your blessing and, uh . . ." She hesitated, and Adam picked up the slack.

"Some assistance from the foundation would be nice," he said brazenly. "You know, we're down here doing the groundwork. We got a committee together."

"A committee?" I asked.

"Oh, yeah," he said. "It's about four of us."

"I see," I said.

"Yeah, you see, Queen brought us all together to act on your behalf," he continued. "But if you could throw a little money this way, that could really get the ball rolling."

"You know how these White folks is," Queen said, adjusting her headwrap. "They speak that money language, so we gotta let them know we speak it too."

"A little money?" I asked. It could see the wheels turning behind her eyes, which no longer looked directly into mine.

"Eighty-four thousand dollars," she said with a dismissive wave of her hand and an overly exaggerated eye roll.

"But that ain't nothing, right?" Adam said. "You got that Roc Nation money, right? I heard you and them got a meeting coming up with the NFL, so there's gotta be some money there. And then you got that Botham Jean Foundation money, so—"

"What do you need eighty-four thousand dollars for?" I interrupted him, resisting the urge to scream at someone—or to end the conversation and walk out.

"I apologize, queen," Queen said. "He can be a bit forward sometimes. That's just what they're asking for downtown. City costs and all that. We were informed that you have a meeting with the NFL later this month, so if they really want to put their money where their mouth is, they could start here. I can put together a little flyer for you to have so you can walk into that meeting with something in your hand. You know, something that states the value and importance of this achievement."

"I know what the value of it is," I replied. "He was my brother. I don't need a flyer to make them see the value of it. But what you're saying is if we want to get the street renamed after Botham, somebody needs eighty-four thousand dollars?"

"That's what they told us," Queen said.

"I see," I replied.

"So, yeah, if we can get the ball rolling on the money side of things," Adam said, "we can bring our committee into the fold and start setting up meetings and things like that."

"And I can put those flyers together for you," Queen reiterated. "To take to the NFL meeting."

"That's fine," I said.

"Great!" Queen said. "We'll be in touch."

"Okay."

Then, just as quickly as they'd entered, they were gone. Perhaps they were off to make the flyers. Or maybe they were going to see what other expenses they could accrue for my foundation. I, on the other hand, decided to make a few phone calls of my own.

My first call was to Dallas City Hall.

"Well," explained a clerk, "it is a little more complicated than it may seem or even ought to be. But it can be done. You just need to get the proposal before the council so that they can discuss it and have a vote on it."

"And the cost?" I asked.

"No cost, per se," he explained. "I'm sure it will cost someone money to reprint their business cards or something like that. But the vote just needs to go before the council."

When I hung up the phone, I was torn. On the one hand, I could not help but feel hopeful about the possibility of having Lamar Steet—a street named after a white supremacist who housed the police department that failed my family—renamed after my brother. On the other hand, it was now glaringly obvious that there were people seeking to profit from my family's tragedy under the guise of helping and honoring us. It then became very important to me to know when "activists" were using Botham's name to honor his memory and when they were using it to honor themselves.

In the days after meeting with Queen and Adam about renaming Lamar Street, I gathered as much information as I could about the renaming process. I even spoke briefly with the mayor. The next time Queen reached out to me was in April, and she wanted my blessing for one of the flyers she had created regarding a speakers' event that include every speaker except for someone from the family.

"I was just hoping you would be so gracious as to speak at our event for the rollout of our committee," she explained over the phone. "Obviously, Adam will speak, but there will be other prominent speakers too."

As I looked at the flyer, I was first struck by the names on the picture and, again, the names that were not there. I was also mildly amused that the flyer looked like it was advertising a hip-hop party. One of the speakers, a prominent civil rights lawyer, looked more like he was going to drop a mixtape than present a court case. That Botham's picture appeared among these seemed to suggest that he was going to give a speech himself. In all, there would be six speakers.

"And how much will you need for this speakers' event?" I asked.

"Oh, just fifty thousand dollars," she replied. "But I'm sure we will figure something out."

The next call was a bit more contentious.

"Can you send me the breakdown for the cost of renaming the street?" I asked.

"Absolutely," Queen replied. "It actually looks like they will need eighty-four thousand dollars to cover any incidentals. But I am sure we can get that covered?"

"Sure," I said. "But I will be looking into other avenues just to be sure we get this project off the ground."

"Understood."

"Also," I added, "is it possible to get me added to your committee? I've been asked by city hall why no one from the family is on the committee."

"Oh, has someone already reached out to you?" she asked, flustered. "We haven't even started our process yet."

"Well," I replied, "the exact message I got is that they were not going to entertain any request until they hear from the Jean family. So someone must have reached out from your camp."

"Oh yes," she stammered. "It does seem that someone from our group contacted them. We can discuss the committee's strategy if that is something that interests you."

"Not now," I answered. "Like I said, I want to pursue some other avenues as a possible backup plan."

"Okay," she said. "Since the money has been confirmed, we're going to go ahead and start reaching out to council members. We'll be in touch."

Before we could talk again, I brought the vote on renaming Lamar Steet before the city council. There were, at first, mixed reactions to the renaming.

"Isn't this an abnormal way to go about changing the name of a street?" one council member asked. "I mean, hasn't it had that name for quite some time?"

Another council member, a woman, stood and asked, "How much is this all going to cost? I mean, it could cost some businesses quite a bit in advertising among other things. And has anyone figured out what it will cost the city?"

Still another older woman stood. "Why are we changing the name at all? I mean, we are all greatly saddened by your loss, Miss Findley, but if we are going to start renaming streets, why not honor one of the many police officers who has died serving this city?" An awkward silence filled the room before Mayor Johnson stood up.

"Listen," Mayor Johnson began, "I'm sure there are many minor inconveniences that may come with changing the street name, but for now, we're only talking about a small portion of that street, yes? I think that if we honor Botham Jean today, we will be honoring someone who is just as worthy, if not more worthy, than some of the other names that grace these street signs. This item requires twelve votes to pass. I am going to be part of that twelve, and I would encourage everyone on this council to give serious thought to being part of that twelve."

In the end, the vote was unanimous. On May 27, 2020, we got the street name below the I-30 highway changed to Botham Jean Boulevard. The only real cost to getting the street renamed was the breakup conversation I would have to have with Queen and Adam. The day after the renaming ceremony, I met them at the same coffee shop where we had our first encounter.

"How could you go behind our backs and get the street name passed?" Adam complained.

"And after all the work we put into getting it done!" Queen chimed in.

"Where was eighty-four thousand dollars supposed to go?" I asked.

"Look, it wasn't about the money," Adam began.

"But it was," I replied. "Because you came to me with a number that sure as hell was not needed to get the job done."

"But I got arrested protesting for your brother!" Adam whined.

"And I got tear-gassed. I think," Queen said.

"And for your arrest and your hard work, what did you want?" I asked. "We got the vote passed. Isn't that what your goal was?

"Yeah, but—" Adam began.

I cut him off. "Or was your goal the right to use Botham's name for your benefit any chance you got? Is that the price you charge for your protest? You should probably advertise that somewhere. Because if your price for protesting is anything but justice, you should go ahead and stay home next time.

"If you are going to do something under my brother's name, do it to honor his memory. Do it because you want to see justice served. Not because you have a block party to throw in his memory. Or because you're making a collection of slain Black men to show off as trophies to people looking to see how woke you are. You sit around acting like Botham's death affected you, until you bleed his name dry and you can move on to the next tragedy. But when you move on to the next tragedy, I will still be dealing with this one— now and forever."

Neither Queen nor Adam was pleased with my remarks.

"I can't believe how ungrateful you are!" Queen said. "And after all that we went through over this."

"All you went through?" I asked.

"Yes!" Adam said. "I had to go and get all of those signatures. And then you just let them snatch that achievement away from us."

"Right!" Queen chimed in. "My son and I were never the same after Botham died."

It was in this moment that I realized they had no true idea what I had gone through when I lost Botham, nor did they seem interested in knowing. They cared not for my pain if they thought they could equate it with their own. If they saw a child stub her toe on a rock, they would scold the rock and forget to comfort the child. If they saw a spider capturing a butterfly, they would squash both in the name of killing the spider, the butterfly's life be damned. They did not truly see Botham; they did not see the innocent life lost. And for that reason, I knew I no longer wished to work with them.

"Oh," I remarked, "I'm so sorry for your loss."

Turning to leave the coffee house, I noticed their stunned faces and open mouths in the reflection of the glass door, and I could not help thinking that they looked like zombies who would devour me if I stayed behind long enough to let them catch me. Whatever their brand of activism, it seemed they only needed something to latch onto, something to feed them with purpose.

As I rode toward the airport to return to New York, I considered that as I toed the precipice of grief, I looked back to find few people trying to pull me back from the edge.

About a week later, I had to read an article in the *Dallas Observer* in which the two prominent members of the Botham Jean Memorial Committee voiced their displeasure at being excluded from the deal. What they failed to mention was the $84,000 I had saved them.

Chapter Eighteen

I opened the window to indulge the smell of the morning winter air, to feel its bitter coldness as it clawed its way past the warmth in the room. I hoped the cold would jolt me awake. Or maybe it would make me uncomfortable enough to finally leave this room, which I had seen little reason to depart from lately. But I needed to be "on" for the day; I had promised to be. It was Christmas, after all. My mother, my brother Brandt, and his father, Bertrum, had flown from Saint Lucia to be here, and they had invited other family members to my house. My favorite way to celebrate Christmas had always been to do it with family, but I especially loved celebrating it with Botham. Since his death, I had found it difficult to celebrate any holiday or birthday. Christmas was especially difficult. But on this third Christmas since Botham's death, I promised my mother I would try.

"Good morning!" my mother said behind me, shattering the silence I had grown accustomed to in my room. My sons rarely ventured in here unless there was some very pressing matter. No one else on earth had any reason to be here. Yet here was my mother, entering my room unannounced as if we were back in Saint Lucia and I was a teenager. A bit annoyed, I had the thought to remind her that this was my house. But I wished her good morning instead.

"We are going to open presents soon," she said with a cheerfulness that almost offended me. I knew what she was trying to do. She wanted to carry on an air of Christmases past. She was going to try and out-cheer my gloom. And I hated her for it.

I opened the window even wider and embraced the bite of winter. I felt the warmth rush out of the room, and in its place came the familiar New York notes of asphalt and exhaust, a hint of cigarette ash left behind by some poor soul who still needed to smoke but was not allowed to do it in his house, and the faintest smell of piss. I imagined that this air took just a bit of the joy out of my mother's mood. But she continued to smile as she set about straightening up my bed. I could not let that happen.

"I'll do that," I said, startling myself with the sound of my own voice. There was an anger there, but it seemed more pronounced from the raspiness that settles in the vocal cords when they are not used for a long time. I cleared my throat.

"Will you?" she asked with the sass afforded her by her Caribbean blood and a couple of college degrees. Her intonation rose, not because she had asked a question but because she already knew the answer to that question.

"I will," I said, trying my best to match her sass. Perhaps I succeeded because she headed toward the door.

"Come down for presents," she said. "The boys are waiting for you."

I remained in the room a while longer, breathing that bitter air and suddenly longing for the air in Saint Lucia. Even if I had grown to love New York, flaws and all, Christmas had become a day when I realized just how very far I was from home. And Botham. I longed to see him, and that longing caused a sinking feeling in my stomach. I looked at my unkempt blankets and sheets.

Go back there. Back to sleep. You can see him there.

"No," I said. Then, as if to prove my own commitment to being antisocial, I shouted, "Jayden! You boys cleaned your rooms yet?"

Do you really even care about that?

"No!" Jareem called back. "I did, but Jayden didn't!"

I sighed as they began to bicker. Their voices became just noise to me. The desire to crawl back into bed was almost irresistible. I felt like a moth drawn to fire. I even took a few steps toward the bed, but a voice stopped me.

"Aren't we going to open presents first?"

I turned to see Jordan at the door with the sweetest look of concern on his face, and I could not help smiling. "Let's make our bed first," I said.

"You didn't make your bed neither," he said.

"You wanna help me?" I asked.

"Okay," he said, shrugging his shoulders. Together, we stripped the bed of its covers and then set about replacing them with clean sheets.

"It looks like a parachute!" Jordan declared as we tossed the fitted sheet on the bed first. I chuckled as I remembered the time my mother taught me to make the bed. I'd thought the same thing. When he was old enough, I'd taught Botham. He never seemed to get the hang of putting the fitted sheet on. Or perhaps he was just content to have me do it for him each time.

By the time Jordan and I finished making the bed, I felt that I might be strong enough to leave my room behind.

I followed my youngest son out of my room, but as he continued down the hall to his room, I only looked past him to the light flooding from his room and into the otherwise dark hallway. I could not go anywhere near that door. Instead, I pictured Botham as a child.

Once, when we were at our childhood home in Saint Lucia, Botham stood in front of my bedroom door and watched me as I readied to leave for college in the United States. I didn't notice the look on his face then, but it must have been a sad one. He was only eight years old. While I looked ahead to the life and future I could make for myself, he tried to grasp life with us being so far away from each other. Ten years later, he and Brandt would regard each other in the same way, the elder looking ahead to his future while the younger tried to fathom an entire sea between them.

For a long while, I stood and stared at my son's open door. We were standing directly in front of each other, but I felt so far away from him.

"Mom, come and see what I did!" Jordan shouted from his room. I did not know if he had made his bed quickly or if I had been standing there for a long time. Perhaps I would have stood there forever if he had not called me. As I entered the hallway, Jayden and Jareem hurried by me.

"I bet I got a PS5," Jareem said to his brother as they made their way downstairs, their footsteps as heavy as five grown men tumbling down those stairs.

"Stop running in this house!" I called after them, but they were already in the living room and rummaging through the piles of gifts.

"Wait until I get down there," I said, though I stood still in the hallway, my eyes closed.

This way. Back to your bedroom.

No. Don't go back there. Go down the stairs. Prepare the house for your family.

Without Botham.

For Botham.

I can't celebrate this holiday without Botham.

You must celebrate it. For Botham.

When I opened my eyes, I was at my bedroom door again.

Maybe, if I try hard enough, I can see Botham in my dreams.

That won't bring him back though.

Then why bother being awake at all?

Allisa. You promised.

I turned and headed back to the stairs, my steps slow and deliberate. I had to focus on putting one foot in front of the other, but finally I made it downstairs.

In the living room, my parents sat beside the Christmas tree we had picked out together. It was both tall and wide. Jaydan and Bertrum had made the greatest effort to get it into the house. Botham might have moved it on his own. The scent of pine and cinnamon from the spiced pinecones that adorned the tree filled the room. Along the decorative fireplace were six stockings hanging with our names printed neatly on them.

Only six stockings. Not seven.

Trying my best to ignore that thought, I approached my mother, who held up a gift for me. I took it, and to my surprise, I began to feel warmer, more at ease.

Maybe I can do this.

There was a lightness to opening the gifts. Laughter came easy. The looks on my sons' faces as they unwrapped surprise after pleasant surprise warmed my heart in a way that it had not been warmed for a very long time.

"Jareem," I said at one point. "Go and get my phone charger from my room."

"What's the magic word?" he said.

"Now," I replied with my mother's sass, but there was so much levity in that sass. The room filled with the music of our shared sense of humor.

When we sat down to breakfast, I was grateful for the meal my mother made. And I was proud to have a house for them to visit and a kitchen full of food that I could feed them. Even the grocery shopping was a fond memory.

Jayden had gone to the grocery store with me the previous afternoon. I'd needed someone to reach the top shelves for me, and he was the tallest. Every time he reached up to get something I couldn't, he reminded me of Botham. His shirt didn't quite fit anymore because of his growing, and that reminded me of how Botham's shirts never fit.

"It's these biceps, sis," Botham would joke. "I was in the gym heavy last week. I figure if I keep working on the arms, no one will notice my stomach is getting bigger too."

I laughed out loud as Jaydan lowered the carton of salt into the cart and his sleeves loosened around his arms.

"Is it the wrong one?" he asked, looking at me quizzically.

"No." I chuckled. "It's fine."

"What's funny?"

"Oh, nothing."

He shrugged, content to see me smile.

On that Christmas Eve, Bertrum led us in a prayer before we sang hymns.

"To Canaan's land, I'm on my way where the soul never dies," Bertrum began to sing, and we with him. "My darkest night will turn to day." It was a song Botham had taught him, and it seemed that the notes poured out of him more clearly than I had ever heard them before. It took all of my strength to sing along with him. "No sad farewells, no tear-dimmed eyes," we sang, though there was not a dry eye among us.

For our next song, Bertrum chose a more upbeat one, and I was grateful. After that, my mother chose to sing "You Are My Strength," and my sorrow would not allow me to get through even the first refrain. I fled upstairs to my room and closed the door behind me. I even locked the door as if the notes would rise from their mouths and follow me up the stairs simply to haunt me.

When I went to sleep later that night, I dreamed that I explained myself to Botham.

"I'm sorry," I said to him. "I could not sing a joyful noise. I could not sing your song."

"By and by, it will get easier," he said.

"No," I said. "It won't. I won't let it."

"Why not?"

"It won't bring you back."

He looked at me with a puzzled expression. Then I awoke and could not fall asleep again.

Christmas morning turned to afternoon, and it became time to prepare our Christmas feast. Aunts and uncles and cousins were beginning to arrive, and the whole house was livelier than it had been in a long time. My mother immediately set about boiling water for the green figs. My aunts cleaned and skinned sweet potatoes. I busied myself with every task I could, so long as it was not a cooking task.

"Do you have everything you need for your lasagna?" my mother asked.

"I hope so," I replied. "The stores are all closed right now." But that would have been a fantastic excuse. If I had thought of it beforehand, I might have left some vital ingredient at the store. Then I would not have been able to make the dish even if I wanted to. And I did not want to. The last time I'd made it was for Botham. I will always remember that Christmas because there was no way I should have seen him at all.

"You're going to drive from Austin to Maryland?" I had asked.

His laugh was so musical as he replied, "No! Of course not. I'm going to Dallas to get some clothes first. Then I'll drive to Maryland."

"That's even worse!" I said incredulously. "You're gonna fall asleep on the road."

"Well, I need clothes."

"Let me get you something. I'll head to the store right now."

"Do you know my size?"

"It's the same as before, isn't it?"

"Sis, I'm a growing young man." He chuckled. "You can't expect me to be the same size as before."

"Fine," I said. "We'll go shopping when you get here."

"Okay."

"Drive safely," I added. "We can't wait to see you, but we want to see you in one piece."

"You're making my favorite, right?" he asked.

"Of course!"

"Then I'll drive extra fast."

"Extra safe."

And now you'll make lasagna without him, I thought as I watched the other women move about the kitchen with joy and purpose. I tried to busy myself in a similar way, but even as I set the water to boil, a lethargy set in my bones.

Do they even understand the importance of this dish?

"Well, do you?" I asked aloud but to no one in particular. My mother looked at me with a puzzled expression while my aunts continued to chat.

"What's wrong?" she asked.

"I don't think I can make this," I said, a quiver setting into my throat, threatening to overtake my entire body.

"Of course you can," my mother said in an encouraging tone. "Only you can."

"I mean, I know I can," I said. "But also, I can't. Not when Bo isn't here."

"If he were here, he would want you to make it," my mother said gently.

"Of course he would want me to make it!" I snapped. My voice became frantic as I tried to fill my throat with words to keep the sobs down. "Because he would be here to eat it. He's not here. If he were here, he would want me to make it. But he isn't here, so he doesn't want me to make it. He can't want me to make it. He—"

"My dear," my mother interrupted, "the only way you are going to move on is if you get back to the things that bring you joy."

"I don't want to move on!" I cried. "Why would I want to move on? Why do you? Why is that so *easy* for *you*?"

"It is not easy," she said. "But it is necessary."

"Why is it necessary?"

"Would you go on with this melancholy the whole of your life?"

"Shouldn't I?"

"The devil would have you do so."

"I don't care about what the devil would have me do."

"But you give him his wish all the same," my mother said matter-of-factly.

"No!" I retorted. "I would give him his wish by dancing around this kitchen, pretending my brother hadn't been killed."

"No, you make a joyful noise to the Lord," my mother explained. "That is how you make the devil mad."

As I watched the steam rise from the pot, I felt the familiarity in my mother's words. Part of me wanted to embrace the truth in what she'd said. There was a familiar light to those words, the memories of the many times Botham had said the same thing. I wanted to reach, to rise toward the light of wisdom. But the weight of his loss was too heavy. And it sank me into the darkness. I could not bring myself to complete the dish. I could only watch the water boil and imagine the process: adding the noodles and straining them; frying the ground beef; putting the stewed tomatoes and paste into the pot; adding the herbs; mixing the ricotta; putting the layers in the pan; baking it; and finally placing it hot and aromatic on the table. Just so Botham would not eat it.

Leaving the pot and water to boil, I turned and walked out of the kitchen.

"Are you okay?" I heard Bertrum say as I passed him for the stairs.

Up the stairs. Down the dark hall. To the closed door.

The coldness of the doorknob did not remind me that I had left the window in my bedroom open. Only the bitterness of the air inside did that. Cold, dark bitterness. Inside, I closed the door behind me and locked it. I did not even close the window. I only crawled beneath the covers and listened to the muffled sounds on the other side of my bedroom door.

My mother continued to converse with my aunts but in hushed tones. I imagined they were trying to figure out what was wrong with me. Maybe they disapproved of my sadness. Maybe they pitied me. Before long, though, they were back to their jovial ways. The doorbell rang, and people entered my home. Sometimes their voices were familiar; sometimes they were not. I assumed they were friends of my parents. Several of them asked about me, then the voices dropped to a hush as someone explained why I was not in attendance. When the conversations trailed off into the kitchen, I wondered if they were speaking ill of me. But when the conversation stayed by the front door or at the foot of the stairs, I knew they were doing much worse than speaking ill; they were pitying me.

I did not want their pity. There was nothing wrong with me. It was the world that was all wrong.

We live in a world where you have to fight to send murderers to jail. Where innocent Black men are killed for existing, and the first instinct of the police departments is to cover their tracks, which they can do far more efficiently than any criminal could. We live in a world where tragedies like these happen every day, and no one feels the need to fix the problem. But the victims are expected to just go on with their lives.

I wasn't going do that. I was determined to feel my pain, and I was determined to figure out a way to make everyone around me feel it too.

We should all feel it every day until a change is made. And if others don't feel the same way about justice, then there is something wrong with them. Not me.

With these thoughts in mind, I curled up under my blankets, and tried as best I could to let the world outside my bedroom fade away. Then I fell into a deep sleep. But I did not dream of Botham. I dreamt of Amber Guyger rotting away in a jail cell, her body shivering in the coldness of the concrete and steel surrounding her.

Chapter Nineteen

Good morning.

These two words can easily be deprived of their meaning. Most times, we say this phrase as a greeting without any consideration to its true message. We often say "How are you?" when we really don't care to engage the actual conversation that could potentially come up as a response to that question. Maybe stating "Good morning!" is a declaration of the state of things.

You might have said, "It is a good morning" to someone on a morning when waking up and going about your usual routine brought you a particular joy. Or perhaps you meant, "Are you having a good morning?" Because when you looked at that person, your care and consideration for her led you to wonder about her well-being. Or perhaps there was an expression on her face that made you hope her day might improve. Maybe you hoped to be the one person who made her day better. And then again, maybe you told someone, "Have a good morning!" And because that person listens to you, your words and advice mean something to them.

Good morning.

Words have a certain power to them.

"Good morning," I said aloud to the world outside my window. Why? Because I wanted to have a good morning. I was beginning to forget what those felt like.

It was a November morning in 2021 when I first began to realize how much of a cloud I had been living under. The civil trial my family and I had longed to bring against the Dallas Police Department had been stalled for over two years. The police reform acts that we had hoped for were dead in the water. Most of all, countless Black men and women were continuing to die at the hands of the police.

In 2019, Atatiana Jefferson was killed in her own home as she was babysitting. The beginning of the pandemic in 2020 saw the deaths of Breonna Taylor and George Floyd. Even the death of Ahmaud Arbery, a race-related killing—though not police-related—weighed heavily upon me.

Every time a murder played out across my television screen and all over social media, I experienced the trauma of losing Botham all over again. With Atatiana's death, I remembered Botham's innocence and ambition as they perished in their own home. When Breonna heaved her last breaths, I heard Botham grumbling in the background of Guyger's 911 call. When George Floyd called out for his mother, I remembered that I should have been there so that Botham wouldn't have died alone. And when I watched Ahmaud being chased by those White men in pickup trucks, I could suddenly and vividly see the hopelessness that must flash before a Black man's eyes before his life is taken, that briefest of moments when he must realize that he will never know what led to his death. Maybe he would think he had actually done something wrong. But what could be so wrong that he had to die? He must have known in that moment that he was being killed for the color of his skin, that these men had deemed themselves judge, jury, and executioner to his crime of being Black in the "wrong" place.

Every new case of police brutality pushed me further into despair. One day, I simply wanted to have a good morning, and I was bold enough to think I could make it happen. So I put those words into the air and walked to my closet to find clothing that would match the beautiful day I wanted to have. I found a caramel-colored blouse to pair with a charcoal skirt and a comfortable pair of heels. I was going into the office briefly that day, then I would head out on a few sales calls. It was best I find shoes suitable for walking.

As I left the house, I discovered that the weather promised a pleasant response to my wish. It was a cool but sunny day, typical of

New York autumns. Saint Lucia will always be home, and I certainly found myself missing the tropical air and blue oceans every now and then. But there is no autumn in Saint Lucia. Not like the ones in New York. Saint Lucia was the family I was born into. New York was the family I had chosen, a dear friend.

I reveled in the cityscape that spread along the horizon as I drove toward the expressway. The two-lane road was lined with various shades of orange and gold. What caught my attention the most were the luscious red leaves flitting about me in the wind as if the trees were waving hello, and I could almost hear them say, "See you soon!"

I stopped at a coffee shop on my way to the office, if only to be outside for a moment to watch and smell the vibrantly colored leaves up close. But the first tree I saw was not like the ones I'd seen on the road; it was filled with only brown leaves, as was the next.

Damn.

I walked for a few blocks more, but still there were only brown leaves.

Maybe it's already too late in the season, I thought. I finally saw one that took my breath away—a broad oak just before the entrance of a park.

There he is. There's my Botham.

I smiled then, having found what I was looking for. Turning back to the coffee shop, I noticed a few more trees with red leaves that it seemed I'd missed.

Funny. How could I have missed these?

As I got closer to my destination, I noticed one tree that nearly appeared to be aflame, so brilliantly did the sun shine through its red leaves.

So sorry I missed you.

Inside, I ordered my usual. Then I sat to await my order and observe the other customers coming and going. A mother in yoga pants and her a daughter bundled up in a scarf and coat that was much too big for her, smiled at each other. The girl held a Frappuccino while the mother waited for her own order.

A few people came and went without ordering anything. They either used the public bathroom or simply stood for a moment and typed on their phones. They must have stopped simply to get warm—the autumn cold is only charming for a little while before it becomes disarming.

There were other patrons who came in to use the free internet. Not nearly enough cups of coffee were purchased for all the bodies that sat at tables, typing away on their laptops. One heavyset woman in dingy clothing with exposed, ashy ankles sat at a table near the door while her service dog lapped up water from one cup and whipped cream from another. Finally, a similarly heavyset man walked in, dragging what seemed to be all of his belongings behind him in a cart.

That must be bae to the woman by the door, I thought as he made a beeline for the restroom. Imagining them applying lotion—him to her ashy ankle and her to his ashy elbows—made me chuckle softly to myself.

Good morning!

After a short while, a young girl in her late teens or early twenties approached with my order. In a ceramic mug. I was only slightly annoyed.

"What a lovely red blouse you have on," she remarked as she set the steaming-hot beverage on the table in front of me. She disarmed me further with her charm and her compliment, softening my complaint.

"I'm sorry," I said. "I ordered that to go."

"Oh!" the girl replied. "I only thought . . . I mean, since you were sitting down—"

"You know what?" I interrupted with a smile. "Don't even worry about it. I have a little time this morning."

The girl smiled gratefully. "Is there anything else I can get for you?"

"No, thank you."

I unbuttoned my jacket and pulled it off so that it rested around the back of the chair. Then I lifted the cup to my lips and blew the steam away as I looked up to steel a glance at the lady and her dog by the door. If Botham were here, we would probably create entire narratives about her and anyone else who walked into the coffee shop. He would have gotten a kick out of the lady and her dog, but not because of the lady, who was mostly plain-looking except for what had to be painfully ashy ankles. But the dog was a rather handsome mixed breed wearing an absolutely charming sweater and cap.

"I don't even think it was her idea to come into the coffee shop," Botham might have said with a chuckle. "The dog has a look that says, 'It's time for an espresso.'"

I took a sip and placed the cup back down before I glanced over at the bathroom door, which now had someone waiting in front of it.

He's still in there, I thought. *That guy waiting may want to seek another option.* I chuckled again, blew on the hot beverage, and took another sip, allowing the hot, sweet liquid to linger on my tongue before swallowing it. Its warmth spread through my chest and then my entire body. It was like a hug but from the inside out, and it reminded me of the big hugs I used to get from Botham. His big arms and broad shoulders made me feel like the little sister sometimes. He was also the person who got me into drinking coffee. He was always so excited when he had a cup or when he was going to get some.

"This woman doesn't have a dog," he might say, holding the cup to his lips to hide a smirk. "It's the other way around: the dog has a human!"

The woman took a seat at one of the tables and, removing a bowl and bottle from a knapsack she carried on her back, she poured a liquid for the dog to drink. It was not water. Perhaps it was tea.

I glanced over at the bathroom door, which still had not opened.

"Maybe he is showering in there," Botham would wonder aloud. "All the while, his wife and dog are waiting."

Soon, I noticed the barista, the same young lady who served me, approaching to the door. She knocked twice and waited. Then she knocked again and looked back to the counter where the other barista—a young, thin Black man with dyed pink hair and a septum piercing—stood. They smirked at each other, and the young girl shrugged her shoulders before returning to the counter. The man who was waiting there had left the shop without my noticing. I looked back to the lady at the door.

You'd better go get your husband!

As I lifted my cup to take another sip, two people walked in, a young man and woman. The man, who was as tall and broad as Botham, wore a deep wine-colored sweatsuit, almost the color of blood. The woman next to him was much shorter but wore a long wool coat that made her look tall.

While they approached the counter, the male barista approached my table. The wide grin across his face indicated that he was quite amused.

"I'm sorry," he said. "Ava and I have a bet going on the color of your shirt. By the way, it's cute on you."

"Okay," I replied curiously. "Thank you."

"Oh, you're welcome! Anyway, Ava says it's scarlet, but I think it's rose. You know, like rose red? I think scarlet is much darker, and I'm usually pretty good about—"

"Actually, it's brown," I interrupted. He raised his brows, glancing down and then quickly back up to me.

"Are you sure?" he asked. "It looks pretty re—"

"Caramel, in fact," I interrupted again, standing to put my jacket back on.

"Like caramel apple?" he reasoned, twisting his lip and furrowing his brow.

"Quite sure," I said. "Can I get this to go?" I picked up the mug and thrust it toward the barista, causing a bit to spill over the sides.

"Oh, sorry about that," he said as if he had caused the spill.

He took the mug carefully, looking both remorseful and confused, then hurried back to the counter. I became agitated, but I was also curious about the bathroom situation. As I made my way over to the door, it suddenly flew open and the man rushed out, having replaced his shirt with a brick-colored sweater. Dragging his cart behind him, he did not even stop to acknowledge the heavyset lady or her dog.

Shame. They could've been cute together.

Ava came to me with my coffee in a to-go cup. She smiled politely and presented the cup, but her eyes were fixed on the collar of my blouse, which peeked out just a bit from my coat.

"Thank you," I said, taking the cup and turning away from her. I walked briskly to the door, and as I passed through it, I looked at the heavyset lady.

"Good morning," I said to her.

"Why, thank you!" she replied.

I buttoned my coat almost to the top as I left the coffee shop and kept it this way even after I entered my car and resumed my drive to work.

It seemed to me that there were more trees with brown leaves or trees that were completely barren as I grew closer to my destination. I was keeping an eye out for more colorful trees when a sudden horn blast grabbed my attention. I looked frantically around as a dark-colored sedan pulled up on my passenger side. The driver rolled down his tinted window to yell at me. He was pissed!

"Are you blind?" he shouted so that I could hear him in spite of my closed window. "You just ran a red light back there!" Then he pulled past me, exceeding the speed limit. I might have waved an apology to him had he not pulled away so quickly.

Did I really miss a red light? I decided to keep my eyes on the road.

Good morning.

I saw that the next intersection had a green signal, so I proceeded confidently through it. The light after that had a yellow signal, but I was confident I would make it. Next was green. Then another green. Then a yellow. Then a strange one. It flashed yellow, but it was at the top of the signal. I proceeded with caution, and someone else blared their horn at me. This time, the car was oncoming and trying to turn left in front of me. I stomped on the brakes, and my car came to a screeching halt in the middle of the intersection.

"What the hell is wrong with you?" a woman screamed out her window. "You don't know how stop signs work anymore?"

"The light is yellow!" I screamed back.

"Are you color-blind?"

She turned, and I proceeded through the intersection rather cautiously. It seemed that every driver and pedestrian was looking at me. Even after I was a mile away, I felt their eyes on me. By the time I arrived at work, I was beginning to calm down, but I was still a bit frazzled.

Stop sign?

"Good morning!" Lydia, one of my coworkers, interrupted my thoughts as I got to the main entrance.

"Hey," I replied.

"I'm just getting something from my car," she explained as she made her way past me. "Hey!" she called back. "Watch out for Amber. She's in a mood. Don't pay her any mind."

I nodded politely and headed in. Reaching my cubicle, I hung my coat on the back of my chair and placed my bag beneath my desk. I did not plan on being there long, just long enough to check some emails and send a few of my own. I had no intention of speaking to Amber. In fact, I figured I would be out of there long before she even thought to come hang by my desk. That was the idea. But she was at my desk before my computer finished starting up.

Damn updates.

"Hey, Lisa!" Amber said as she leaned against the entrance of the cubicle. "That shirt is cute! I bet I know what your favorite color is."

"Do you?" I said with a workplace smile.

"Of course!"

"Go on."

"I mean, it's obvious your favorite color is red. You wear it every day!"

"Do I?" I asked.

"Yes! But don't worry. It looks good on you. I especially love this shade." She tapped me on the shoulder to indicate the color of the blouse.

"Well, this *shade* is brown," I clarified. "And brown is, in fact, my favorite color."

Amber frowned, puzzled. "No," she said, "this is definitely red. Did you get dressed in the dark or something?"

I looked down to see that my shirt was indeed red. I smiled sheepishly. "Oh, I must have." I tried to laugh off my mistake. "You know, the time change is a pain in the ass."

"Isn't it?" Amber laughed. "Why are we even still doing that?"

"Right?"

"Did you see Lydia on the way in?" Amber asked with a discerning grin. "Didn't she look terrible? Because babies don't care about daylight saving time. Her little one's sleep schedule is all messed up."

She continued gossiping about one person or another, and I nodded and laughed with her. But my mind was on the color of my shirt. I kept looking down at it.

How had I not noticed that?

Once I was alone again at my desk, I tried to focus on my work. I opened one email and then stood to go to the restroom. There, where the florescent lights were brightest, I saw that my shirt was unmistakably red.

Not scarlet or rose. Botham red.

Part of me was quite pleased with this color name. Another part of me wondered how I could have made such a mistake. Still, another part of me tried to recall what colors were in my wardrobe.

I don't know when it happened, but almost my entire wardrobe had become filled with red articles of clothing. In fact, I didn't think I had anything new that wasn't red. And most of my older clothing had become too big for me. I began to shake from this realization, and even putting my coat on could not stop my trembling.

"It is freezing in here, isn't it?" Lydia remarked as she walked by and saw me bundled up.

"Yes," I lied. Then I picked up my bag and left.

As I drove to my sales call, my mind wandered back to the first grand jury indictment. That was when I first began wearing red. We all did—the whole family and Botham's friends too. Botham's Army, I called us. We wore red because it was his favorite color. We wore it because it represented his zeal for life. We wore it so everyone would know how passionately we would fight for his justice. I started wearing it then, and it seemed that I had never stopped wearing it. I had worn red so much that people thought it was my favorite color. Even more than that, I had almost forgotten that my favorite color is brown. I had nearly become blind to red. My mind, once again, was not my own. Or perhaps it hadn't been mine from the moment I found out about Botham's murder.

A horn blared, and I realized that I had run a red light. It blared again, and I realized that I had stopped at a green one. Before long, my entire body shook so that I no longer trusted my hands to steer me in the right direction. The car seemed to drive by its own volition. Meanwhile, I felt the same way I had on my sales call at the apartment complex: my body would not do what I told it to do. It turned left when I wanted it to turn right. It mistook red lights for green lights. When I finally pulled into a parking lot, I turned off the engine and sat quietly in the car for a long time.

Deep breath.

I opened the door and stepped out of the car.

Another deep breath.

I looked around and found that I was not where I needed to be for the sales call. But the place was familiar. I'd begun walking toward the building when I realized why it was familiar. I was at my doctor's office. I continued to the main entrance, pulled open the glass door, and stepped inside.

I do not remember saying much to the receptionist. I definitely did not have an appointment. Nevertheless, I was only in the waiting room a short while before my physician came out to see me. She had a sympathetic look on her face.

"Good morning," she said.

* * *

"No, you are not fine," Dr. Shelton said as she looked me in the eyes. I saw kindness radiate from her. And concern. I could not imagine what she saw radiating from me.

"Post-traumatic stress," she continued. "Your body is reacting as if you are still experiencing your brother's death. What things have you been doing to process what happened?"

"Things?" I asked, still looking at the kindness in her eyes.

"Have you talked to anyone? Maybe taken time away from work?"

"No."

"No to both questions?"

I looked away from her.

Was I supposed to?

I did not ask the question aloud because deep down I knew that I should have. I should have talked to someone. I should have done anything to keep the shaking from settling into my bones, to keep the despair from settling into my soul. For three years I had let this suffering become a part of me. It was easy to ignore that suffering.

"I have had too much to take care of," I explained. "So many things to get done."

"I see," Dr. Shelton responded. "What are some of these things?"

"I mean, there were the funerals," I began.

"*Funerals?*"

"Yes, we had two. One in Texas and one in Saint Lucia, where Botham is buried."

"Okay."

"Then there was the trial. The foundation. The requests from organizations, people wanting to hold benefits for him, do documentaries. Some people are earnest, but some people want to take advantage of his name. I have to protect him from that."

"You alone?"

"Who else? I am the only one here."

"That certainly sounds like a lot."

"Yes, it is. You see, I don't know when I would have had time to do anything else."

"Well you have to make time," Dr. Shelton remarked. "You're falling apart."

"I feel that," I said, remembering the bouts of shaking and the loss of appetite.

"How have you been sleeping?"

"As much as I can," I replied. "That's one thing I haven't had trouble doing. Or at least I have been in the right place to do it."

"Finding it hard to get out of bed some days?"

"Sometimes."

"Mhmm," Dr. Shelton uttered pensively as she jotted something down on a clipboard. There was a long silence, and I felt a need to fill the silence.

"You need to take care of yourself. You can't be here to handle things for Botham if you aren't here for yourself."

I nodded in agreement.

"And you need to find healthy ways to process your grief," she added.

"How could you process losing someone close to you?" I asked. "And in the way that it was done?"

"Do you mean how would I process it?" Dr. Shelton asked.

"Yeah, that's what I said."

"That's not what you said. You asked me how *could* I."

"Did I?"

"Do you think you literally can't process it? Or do you think that you need permission to do so?"

"Permission?" I asked. "From whom?"

"I don't know," Dr. Shelton replied. "Listen, I am going to give you something to get you out of bed in the morning. And I want to give you something for your shakes. That's what I can do for you physically. As for processing your trauma, I strongly suggest you find a therapist to talk to. I know a good one."

I only nodded. I was stuck on one word.

Permission.

Rising from the chair, I took the prescription note from her and headed for the door.

"Also," Dr. Shelton added, "and I cannot stress this enough, no work! Not for a whole week. I'll write you a note for your employer."

I knew I was going to have to call work and explain what happened, but the entire ride home I could only think about one thing.

That doctor must be crazy. What would I need permission for? To process my own trauma? I don't need permission to do that.

Then why haven't you done it yet?

Because I have been too busy. Because I have three boys to take care of and a job to hold down and two organizations to maintain. But if I wanted to take time, I would.

Would you?

Yes.

Chapter Twenty

I went to see Melody one week after the referral from my physician. I realized that Dr. Shelton was right about being there for Botham.

Melody had kind brown eyes and a smile so full and innocent it had a childlike quality. I would have believed that she was much younger than I if I did not already know better.

Her office was neat and inviting. Entering, I saw that her desk was against the far wall near a large window with blinds and half-drawn curtains. The desk was simply decorated: her laptop in the center, a framed picture that faced the chair, a cup of pens, and a small money tree plant.

She's kind and neat. So far, so good.

In the center of the room was a wide area rug beneath a small glass coffee table displaying a few pamphlets and magazines. Around the table were two thick armchairs and a small sofa to match. The smell of lavender filled the air, and I felt at ease in spite of myself. When Melody invited me to sit, I chose one of the armchairs because it looked comfortably restrictive. Nevertheless, when I sat down, it did not keep me from shaking, nor did it keep my legs from bouncing.

Great! Now she'll know something is wrong with you.

"How are you?" Melody asked with a smile.

"I'm good," I replied.

"You have had a bit of time off." Her intonation rose, signaling a question, but she also seemed to know the answer to the question. I considered pointing this out but immediately thought better of that.

"Yes," I said. "Longest vacation I've had in a while." I laughed uneasily. Melody, however, had the most effortless laugh. I was almost envious. It had been year since I'd laughed like that.

"So," Melody began, "what have you been doing to pass the time?"

"Well," I replied, "I'm here."

More effortless laughter from Melody. "Yes, you are. And what else?"

"Well, the doctor said I should be taking it easy. So I've been doing that."

"Resting?"

"Yes."

"And how is that going? I mean, how are you sleeping?"

"It's okay," I said. "It could be better."

"Are you using anything to help you sleep?"

"Like drugs?"

"Or not like drugs. Music perhaps? Maybe you read before bed?"

"I keep the TV on."

"Anything in particular?"

"*Friends.*"

"Oh?" Melody said, seemingly unsurprised. "Tell me about *Friends.*"

"I like it because it's predictable."

"Do you usually prefer shows that are predictable?"

"Well, I've seen it before. Lots of people rewatch shows they've seen before."

"Are you watching any new shows?" Melody asked.

"Not these days."

"I get it. Not a lot of good new shows on."

"I mean, I don't know."

"So you go to sleep to *Friends*?" Melody asked.

"Yeah, it reruns on TV Land for most of the night."

"Do you keep it on through the night?"

"It's good background noise," I remarked.

"And predictable," Melody added.

"And predictable," I repeated. Melody was quiet for a brief time. I became a bit uneasy with the silence, so I filled it. "There are no gunshots in friends. No surprises. If I wake up in the night, I know what sounds I can expect to hear."

"That makes sense." Melody offered more silence and stared at me with attentive eyes. I tried to think of something to fill that silence again.

Does she want me to go on? Should I change the subject?

I looked around at the neatly placed minimalist decor. My eyes settled on a large, plain vase of pampas grass. I thought to explain what it was like to wake up in the middle of the night to the shocking news that Botham had been killed. But she did not ask. So I sat with the uncomfortable silence. At least, I was uncomfortable. Melody looked just as tranquil as she had been when she'd greeted me in the waiting room. I was grateful when her lips parted, and she changed the subject. Sort of.

"What else have you been doing?" she asked.

"What else?" I could feel my patience waning. "Eating. What else should I be doing?"

"Eating is good," Melody said, unfazed by the changing tone in my voice.

"Of course eating is good."

"Have you been eating well-balanced meals?"

"Does anyone?" I responded. "Have you?"

"I only ask because your sweater seems a bit big on you."

I looked down and tugged on the sleeves. "I'm sorry."

"That's okay. You have been through a lot. You're entitled to some anger."

"And impatience?" I smiled sheepishly.

"And impatience," Melody assured me. "I don't know if you have noticed any changes in yourself, but usually sleep and diet are the first things to go by the wayside when we are grieving. How long has it been since Botham died?"

Botham died? No . . .

"Since Botham was *killed*?" I emphasized.

"Yes," Melody said without wavering. "Since Botham was killed."

"Almost three years." I tugged more emphatically on my sleeves and shifted in my seat.

"Would you mind telling me how it happened?"

"What is there to tell?" I snapped. "It was all over the news. It's probably all over YouTube."

"I know," she said. "But I haven't heard the details in your words. Your words are the ones that matter in here."

"He was murdered," I said.

How are those words?

"He was murdered by a police officer while he was eating ice cream," I continued. "Eating ice cream."

I looked away to the pampas grass. I considered looking at Melody, but I worried that she might be looking directly at me, observing my reactions, making judgments about the way I was talking, the tremor in my voice, the ache at the back of my throat. Did she know that I felt it? I even felt the well of water at the corners of my eyes.

But that's not about to happen.

"How did you find out?" Melody asked.

"I got a call. While I was sleeping."

There. Now you know why I watch Friends to go to sleep. Happy now?

But Melody didn't comment on that. Instead, she seemed content to let me continue talking, and it was only after I finished discussing my frustration with the Texas Ranger prior to the trial that she made any kind of observation.

"Three years is a long time, huh?"

"It still feels like it just happened," I said.

"That's why you've been shaking," Melody added. "Have you been shaking the whole time?"

"It feels that way," I replied.

"Have you been dealing with any other difficulties?"

"A divorce," I said.

"Divorces are hard even when they're amicabile."

"It wasn't.

"And you juggled that along with the trial and everything?"

"I waited until after the trial for the divorce, but we separated for a year leading up to it."

"So you really were quite busy. No wonder it took you so long to come see me." She smiled genuinely. I smiled back wryly.

"I did not know you," I said.

"I know! That must have made things all the more challenging."

She was being humorous, but I was not in the mood. "I didn't know I was looking for you," I said.

"Well, better late than never, right?" Melody said, standing to signal an end to the meeting. "We all grieve in our own time. As long as it's actual healing that we're doing, it doesn't matter how long we take. Until next time?"

"Sure," I said, standing to take my leave.

Actual healing. What does she mean by that?

The next time we met, Melody's first question was a bit surprising.

"Is there any unfinished business that you had with Botham before he died?" I was taken aback by the question, and for a while all I could do was stare at a pamphlet on the coffee table between us.

Five stages of grief, it said. *Are there only five stages? Sounds simple. Five steps and then you're done.*

"Allisa?"

I looked up at her and thought to mention that I was supposed to give Botham hell over his forgetting to tell me he loved me during our last conversation. And perhaps I owe him that. But I said something else instead.

"His entire life was unfinished business," I said. "I planned to grow old with him. That was unfinished business. He was going to have my nieces and nephews, and they were going to call me 'Auntie.' That was unfinished business. Did I have some? You bet. An entire lifetime—" I caught myself before my voice could crack and the tears could come.

I took a deep breath and continued. "One thing they don't prepare you for in a trial for murder is how that verdict doesn't bring your loved one back. You spend so much emotional energy hoping and praying for the right outcome, for the just verdict. But when the judge reads the verdict and the end of the process has come, you're left with the realization that the verdict didn't bring him back. So what's the use in thinking about 'unfinished business'? Why wonder what I would say if he were still here? I can't get him back, can I?"

Melody allowed the silence to linger for a while as though she wanted to be sure I did not have more to say. Then she asked, "What kinds of things have you been doing to heal from your trauma?"

"Well, I began the Botham Jean Foundation. I think that keeps him not only in my memory but in the collective memory. We have a red-tie gala in his memory every year. His favorite color was red, so we wear it in his memory."

"Is that what you're doing," Melody said, pointing to my blouse, which was a bright shade of red. I smiled sheepishly. "Do you often wear that color?"

"No, I usually wear earth tones," I said but stopped myself, remembering how much red was in my closet. "Well, I guess I have been wearing red a lot more lately."

"It's your mourning color," Melody remarked.

"Morning?" I asked.

"Most people wear black when they mourn. But not you. You have been mourning for three years, haven't you?"

"Shouldn't I be?" I asked.

"Nobody can tell you how to mourn," Melody said. "But it has to be clear to you that you're doing that. It seems you have done a lot of things to mourn. What kinds of things have you done to heal?"

"What do you mean?" I asked. "Those things are as much for me as they are for Botham."

"They're not," Melody replied. "Mourning requires that you acknowledge the pain. Sometimes we open old wounds when we mourn, but there is nothing wrong with acknowledging the pain. You just can't do that and heal with the same actions. Mourn all you want, but make sure you take time to heal too."

"How do you know that I haven't?" I asked.

"Well, for starters, you're just now coming to see me, and if your shakes are any indication, you're doing it under duress. But like I said, better late than never. The second thing is your outfit."

"What's wrong with my outfit?" I asked.

"Well, you're still wearing red," Melody explained.

"What's wrong with wearing red? It was Botham's favorite color."

"I know. You told me. When you wore it last week."

"I still don't see what the problem is."

"What is your favorite color?"

"Brown," I said.

"Why aren't you wearing that?" Melody asked. "When was the last time you bought something that color? When was the last time you bought something that was for you, not Botham?"

I thought for a long while before I replied, "I don't know."

"Mourning and healing are not the same thing," Melody said.

"How should I know the difference?" I asked.

"Mourning is what you do for Botham. Healing is what you do for yourself. Whenever you intend to do one or the other, ask yourself who you're doing it for. And answer honestly."

"What should I do to heal myself?" I asked.

"That's a good question. Maybe you could start by wearing some shirts in a different color?"

Melody smiled warmly again, and I tried to smile back. I just wasn't so sure I agreed. It wasn't until I got home that evening and looked in my closet that I began to understand her.

I am losing myself in mourning, I thought. What would it mean to lose myself completely this way? And what should I do to heal? It occurred to me that mourning came quite naturally to me. Doing for Botham came naturally.

I am his big sister. I always made sure he was good. In both life and death, I will always make sure he is good.

And this was true for most, if not all, of the people in my life.

My sons. Even my ex-husband.

But it was also true that I had to tend to myself. I don't know why Melody's words got through to me the way they did. Perhaps I had always known that the things I had been feeling were not normal, but I just wasn't ready to let go of anything that felt like a part of Botham. To stop myself from shaking, to allow myself to laugh, to enjoy Botham's favorite holiday traditions without him were somehow a betrayal of Botham.

These were some of the ideas that Melody pointed out to me, and they seemed to ring true. It was also true that no one had ever talked to me with the purpose of helping me heal. The people around me were either oblivious to my pain or they were grieving with me. And some people, it seemed, were trying to use me. I did not realize how much I needed to talk to someone until I met Melody. And now I was aware that I needed to build myself back up. I was unsure what that looked like, so I needed to figure some things out. In the meantime, I would start by buying some new clothes.

* * *

"He was pissed with me," I explained to Melody at our next session. "My husband was pissed with me that he didn't get the job. As if it were up to me to apply and show up to the interview for him."

"I see," Melody replied. Perhaps I expected her to place some kind of value judgment on the circumstances. Perhaps I needed her to. But she asked a question instead.

"Have you given more thought to what you can do for you?"

"Well, that divorce was for me," I replied.

"It certainly wasn't for him. But even that isn't a healing act. You only got away from the thing that was hurting you. An important step, no doubt."

"Divorce wasn't enough?" I asked with an air of irony.

"Depends on what you have done since then. I don't know of many pains that don't require some act to remedy it."

"Not every pain has a remedy," I retorted.

"Do you have an example?" Melody asked.

"Botham can't come back from his pain."

Melody sighed and looked at me sympathetically. "No, he can't. But you can."

"Why should I? Why should I get to heal when Botham can't?"

"Is that what has been bothering you?"

I frowned and crossed my arms. Feeling like I had somehow been walked into a trap, I did not respond to her question.

"What else do you think is unfair about Botham's death?"

"Everything!" I snapped.

"Tell me."

"The fact that his killer will be free in a few short years is unfair. That he died alone while she had all of her friends and colleagues around her was unfair. That I couldn't be with him. That God took him instead of me. He was good—so good. Far better than me. He would never question God, but you should hear the thoughts I have had since . . ." I trailed off, and we both listened to my heavy breathing until I calmed down.

"Do you think you deserve to heal?" Melody asked. "Or are you afraid that healing—wearing your favorite color instead of his, transitioning from doing things for Botham to doing them for yourself—will mean that you are letting Botham go?"

The shaking became very pronounced throughout my whole body. I did not even try to restrain it.

"I have to go," I said.

Chapter Twenty-One

"Just follow my movement," Melody said as she held her index finger up to me and moved it back and forth.

"Not hypnosis. It's EMDR, Eye Movement Desensitization and Reprogramming." That is what she wanted to try with me. EDMR is a relatively new technique by which the patient learns to focus on a traumatic memory while experiencing typical eye movements. Doing these exercises are supposed to reduce the vividness and emotion of the traumatic memory. I was skeptical of the procedure, but not because I didn't think Melody could help me navigate my own trauma. I was skeptical because I knew that she was up against every trauma I had experienced in the four years since Botham's death. Every new instance of brutality against unarmed Black people was a new trauma for me, even if the police were not always involved. George Floyd reminded me that the police had neglected to administer aid to Botham. The video of Ahmaud Arbery's murder gave me a brief glimpse into Botham's last moments. Because there was no body cam footage for Botham, I could not help feeling that Ahmaud and Botham had the same thoughts when they were realizing that their bullet wounds were fatal. Breonna Taylor died in her own home, where she was supposed to be safe. Atatiana Jefferson had many more years of life to live, so much to offer the world in her own pursuit of education. But she was robbed of that life. More and more, I was beginning to feel that Botham would have wanted me to be a voice for them. In the wake of their tragedies, though, I could do nothing but feel their intense weight pulling me downward.

Because I had been meeting with Melody for three months and was still shaking, I think her goal was to desensitize me. Not only to the trauma I had experienced, but to the traumas that had been awakened in me and the traumas that might still lurk in the inevitable tragedies yet to take place. Melody assured me that she could reprogram my thinking so that I would stop feeling distressed by the memory of Botham being killed. It sure sounded like hypnosis or some other kind of crackpot method to me. But I needed to try something because I was not only feeling the trauma of losing Botham every day, I was also feeling that trauma every time a new act of police brutality was inflicted on another Black life. I felt like I couldn't heal because the wound was being reopened several times a year. I would not ignore the issue; I couldn't. Because it had already cost me too much. And yet, I had to stop shaking. I could not go through life every day feeling this pain. I would not survive that. As it was, I was still having to drag myself out of bed.

So I did as Melody asked. I went back to her office of my own volition. I went back because she was a welcoming spirit. And she had been right about so many things. I didn't know if this strange method was going to work, but I was willing to try it. As she held up her index finger and moved it back and forth, I watched it. And I waited for the pain and the shaking to go away. But first I had to relive that trauma.

Melody's movement was slow and deliberate. She spoke in a calm, soothing voice. Perhaps I only imagined that she put up a second finger. Then a third. And a fourth. By the time she put up a fifth finger on the same hand without unfolding her thumb, I knew my mind was playing some sort of trick on me. Then the room faded away and I saw even more.

Today is a good day. A beautiful day for a run. As I head out the door, the sun shines brightly. Small tufts of clouds drift slowly in the deep blue sky. A light breeze stirs about me. I inhale a deep breath of this warm afternoon air and bound from my porch, down the walkway, and out onto the road. With each foot that pounds the road and carries me forward, I become more invigorated. Today will certainly be good for a longer run out of the neighborhood.

I head down the road, past my neighbors' homes and toward the tree-lined roads ahead. My breaths pull the life force from the air all around me, take it into my lungs, and fills them. My lungs feed that life force to the blood that courses through my veins. My veins carry that energy into my legs. My legs move me across the earth. Faster and faster until my neighborhood fades behind me and I am surrounded on all sides by trees. Life-giving, life-affirming trees that breathe in my exhales and offer me more of this life force to power my body. I feel that I can run for miles.

For a moment, my jog becomes a sprint, and it seems that the world shrinks before me. I can conquer the whole of its lands with just my two feet. I breathe a bit harder and faster to fuel my body. Just another mile ahead and I will transcend one realm of life. Then I will stand before the larger highway with unlimited potential. Maybe I will turn north. Maybe I will see just how far my legs can carry me. I might run to Savannah. Or Charleston. Raleigh or Richmond. D.C. or Philadelphia. My ancestors made that run when every gun in the South would have tried to stop them. What could stop me?

Or maybe I will head east. There is so much earth east of here. Everything is east. I could run to Louisiana or Texas. Arkansas or Missouri. Maybe I would make it to the Rocky Mountains. Or maybe even California. I once heard that's where the Black man went to spread his wings once upon a time. Now we can spread our wings wherever we desire. Can't we?

Or maybe I will head south. Run through Florida until I get to the end of the earth. Then I can look out into the ocean that brought my ancestors here. Look up at the night sky with the same stars they once looked at. Then I can fill this breath, these lungs, that blood within me and think that they had it too. Maybe I will look up at that sky and whisper to their spirits, "I made it. I'm here because you were here first. And that life you lived is in my veins, but it was not lived in vain."

As I approach the highway, I look across its four lanes and decide to head south. Across this wide expanse, where cement masons might have whistled dixie as they sought to connect these bluffs to the rest of Georgia, I find for myself a small haven to complete a circuit before I turn around and head home. A small cluster of trees welcome me to the small neighborhood, and I follow the road as it turns east. There are more trees, but then I cross an intersection and beautiful house on my left. Then another on my right. From this second house I can see through to the boats docked on the river, and I think that I would like to own a home like this one day. Today, I am only jogging through, but on another day, perhaps soon, I will be home when I cross that highway.

Stopping to catch my breath at the next house, I look closer and see that it is not quite a whole house yet.

Maybe this one is for me, I imagine as I take a step toward it. It is always a marvel to see things being created. As I look through the large opening where a window will one day be and then walk across the threshold that will eventually hold a door, it is difficult for me to imagine what this whole thing will look like when it is done. Somehow, each section of the skeletal structure looks too small to be a whole room. Will a living room go here? Will a child chase their siblings through that hall? Can an entire Thanksgiving meal be served in that room over there? Looking up, it is even more difficult to think that a ceiling will divide this floor from one above it. Where will the stairs go? Or maybe this is all one floor.

Behind the house is a dock like the other ones along this river. Only, there is no boat here yet. I wonder what it would be like to walk out of my back door and jump into my boat. I would get in my boat and ride it all the way to the Atlantic Ocean if I could. Maybe I would find some big fish, something to feed my whole family. Then I would come back up this river, around the bends, and dock in my backyard. How cool would that be?

For moment, I imagine that I have gone back in time to this moment before I had anything. Then, at any moment, I could jump back into my time machine and go to where my house is all built up. As I head back to the front of the house, I feel refreshed. Renewed. Like I have some new dream to aspire to. Turning back on the road, I continue my run, the air filling my lungs and fueling my muscles even better than before.

The road curves, and I feel impelled to conquer it at full speed. I breathe a bit faster, a bit deeper. I feel my legs begin to stretch out *over the earth as my feet find places farther and farther ahead of me. I recall my days on the football field.*

Who couldn't I chase down now? *I think.* A wide receiver would be helpless against strides like these.

I find myself soaring in my memories, in my past ambitions of being a pro football player. I am only aware of the wind in my face, the ground below me, and my feet, which push it farther and farther behind me. So gone am I in these thoughts, that I do not notice a vehicle on the road with me until a man's voice shouts to me.

"Stop!" he yells, shattering the images in my imagination. "You stop right there!"

I look over my shoulder to see a white truck behind me. One White man with a red beard and a pale, gleaming scalp littered with wisps of red hair on top of it scowls at me. He must have been the one who thought he could command me to stop. I realize that I do not have to stop. Even more so than that, I realize I probably should not stop. I can think of few experiences—real, on the news, or fictional—that ended well when two strangers follow someone and force them to stop. I can think of no experiences when the strangers were White and the victim was Black. I also remember that I have just run south of where those masons used to whistle Dixie, my heart pumps harder. My thoughts race frantically in my mind. I am in my fullest stride, but I begin to think that I can run even faster. I must. Or they are going to kill me with their truck.

Run, nigga! Run!

I begin to think of the ancestors who ran North from slavery. Past Savannah and Charleston. Past Raleigh and Richmond. Past D.C. To Philadelphia. Only, they were being chased by a few horses. I am being chased by hundreds of them, all reigned to this white pickup truck, which twentieth century Black people always knew to stay away from around these parts. And here I am. In the twentieth century. Being chased by red-headed White men. In a white pickup truck. Just south of where the masons once whistled Dixie.

My legs begin to buckle beneath me. I try to breathe in more air, but I can't fit anymore in my lungs. The white pickup pulls ahead of me and comes to a stop. And an old man with a white beard and white tufts about his ears jumps out and starts walking toward me. I have to make it back north. I turn on a dime and head in the opposite direction. For a brief moment, it occurs to me that I am imagining things. I hope that I am. But I would rather look crazy than be dead. And that White man looked pissed.

The trees overhead blot out the sun and still the air. My breaths are fleeting. The energy does not course through my veins the way that I need it to, but I must make it home. They have to turn their truck around. That should give me a little time to put ground between us. When a black pickup pulls in front of me, it does not immediately occur to me that he is on their side. Only that he is in my way. I find a burst of energy to get around his truck just before he blocks the road entirely. When he turns to pursue me, I know that I am not imagining things. They are really after me.

"You ain't gettin' away that easily!" he cries behind me as he shifts into gear. His tires squeal against the road as he reverses into his driveway. Then his engine roars as he returns to the road behind me. Realizing that his car had emerged from his driveway, it occurs to me that maybe the entire neighborhood is after me. The road seems to encroach on me from both sides, and any thought of making a shortcut through one of these yards or begging someone in the community to help me fades along with the energy from my body. The truck grows nearer and nearer. I cannot make it to the end of this road. I cannot even make it across that highway—let alone to Savannah or Charleston. Raleigh or Richmond. D.C. or Philadelphia.

As the roar of his engine fills my ears and the heat of his engine warms my back, I turn suddenly onto a side road, and his truck skids to a stop past the intersection.

More time, *I think.* That gives me a little more time.

I look ahead to see if this new road leads all the way through the neighborhood.

If there is a God above, this road won't end in a cul-de-sac.

Already, I can hear the black truck engine roaring in the distance.

Why? Why are they doing this?

I wish this road would carry me home.

As my legs begin to cramp and my lungs begin to ache, I look to the side of the road for some place of refuge. There are none, but I must stop. Heading to a large tree at the edge of someone's front lawn, I hope that someone and any of his family are gone for the day. I lean against the tree and place my hands above my head. That's where coach always said to put them when you need to catch your breath. I take several breaths and look in the direction from which I came. I cannot hear the engine roar, but I do see the truck driving slowly. Attentively. He must be checking every yard.

Looking up the road, I see the white pickup turn left and head toward me.

Shit.

I look at the house near me. I couldn't break in and hide. That would be like hiding from a bear by hiding in its den. I am going to have to outrun them.

I take a few more deep breaths and recall my football training.

I am built for this. I can do this.

With new resolve, I turn back toward the black truck and begin to sprint. Now I can hear the roar of engines before and behind me. As I approach the black truck, I dodge quickly to the left and run around it, causing the driver to screech to a halt.

Yes.

With the black truck facing the wrong direction behind me, I look ahead to the intersection I am approaching.

If I can make it there, I will be on the street that got me here. If I can just make it back to the highway, maybe they will stop chasing me. If I can make it . . .

My thoughts are interrupted by the sound of the white truck pulling closer behind me. I can feel its gravity at my back. And just when I think the truck will crush me beneath it, they pass me on my right. The old man is in the bed of the car, yelling something inaudible at me. They stop several yards ahead of me, and all of my strength leaves my body. I slow to a jog. As I get closer, the driver side door swings open and the red-bearded man exits.

I can get past him.

There is no strength left in me. Only hope. I will myself to a sprint toward the man, hoping to juke him in one direction or another.

He is old and fat. What would my coach have said if I let a dude like him catch me?

Then he pulls out a shotgun.

Juke right. No. Left. Get past him before he can swing the gun around. Too late. He is already pointing it toward you. Get behind the truck. Wait, find a tree. No trees. Too late. I passed one. The stop sign is too skinny. The house, too far away. Truck. Get behind the truck. The old man is on top. Run. But I can't. Run, nigga! But I can't. Shit. Close the distance. Grab him. Get the gun.

Boom!

The world goes silent. I feel a punch in my chest, but it is not like any punch I have ever felt anywhere else before. It feels like a punch from God.

But you're still alive. Fight. Swing. Hit his face. Again. Make him drop it. Hit him. Again.

Boom!

I don't hear the second shot, but I feel it in my chest, and it takes the weight out of me. I feel like I am floating in water or wafting away on a cloud. I try to wrestle the gun away from him. But I cannot feel my hands. I can see them grabbing him. They swing and punch him one last time. Then they hold on to him for dear life.

Boom!

My eyes search frantically for help. For someone. Anyone. Please. Come from the house. Come down the street. Come from the sky. See what has happened. I look to the truck and see the old man with the white beard and white tufts around his ears. He is pointing a gun at me too.

Run. Run like you were always taught to do. Run like you love to do. Use those legs God gave you. The legs He filled with so much strength. Use those feet God made faster than most. You are gonna be a star with those feet. A football star.

I feel my whole body drift away from his. I see my legs carry me seven steps away from him.

Then I look up to the sky.

Try as I might, I cannot look away from it.

I see a few faces. One is the angry face of a White man with a red beard. The second is a police officer. I think he is here to save me, but he passes me to console the killer.

Then I saw Melody's face. And the four fingers she held up. I remembered the first time I saw the video of Ahmaud Arbery being chased through that neighborhood. He neither knew the men who chased him nor the reason they were after him. He only knew he had to run as fast as he could. When they finally cornered him, he realized he had run as far as he could. His legs could carry him no longer. When I saw those men shoot him, I remembered that Botham had so little time to process what was happening to him.

I could hear Botham groaning on the 911 call that released to the news media. I told myself I shouldn't listen to it, but I just had to. I wanted to know if it was truly him on the phone; if he cried out for help; if he suffered. The groans I heard in the background tore my heart into a million pieces. I could not bear to listen to him, but I still had to. I even longed to see him in his last moment, but there was no visual of his last moments. Ahmaud Arbery's video became that for me.

* * *

Melody's smile was warm and comforting.

"How are you doing?"

"I saw my brother in Ahmaud Arbery," I replied. "When the police showed up, they didn't even help him. Isn't that what they're supposed to do? Help us? But he got no CPR while he lay there with a bullet wound. In fact, while he lay there writhing and bleeding, the police officers went over to check on the shooter. They did the same to Botham."

"I know," Melody said. "I know this is painful for you. But keep going."

Her hand continued to wave in front of me, and the room faded again.

I'm tall. I know that. Six feet, four inches. And I'm big. One hundred eighty pounds. All muscle. I can move a whole lot, and it takes a lot of force to move me. I know that. But I'm not that kind of guy. I know when you see me, you see a big Black man. Looks like he can play basketball or football. Big ol' Southern-grown, soul-food-eating Black man. I know that. But I'm not that kind of guy. I love the whole world, and the world loves me. I look like a fighter, but I'm not that kind of guy. I'm a lover. And that is how my day starts, with me loving the whole wide world.

My friend lets me borrow her Mercedes truck. Ooh, what a great day it's gonna be. I'm gonna get in that Mercedes and drive it all over Minneapolis. Just gonna be a Mercedes man for the day. And it's good that it's a big truck—an SUV, actually. That's good because I'm a tall guy. I need all of the leg room and all of the headroom that Mercedes has. It has a whole lot of other things on the inside too. I go outside to that car, dark blue like Lake Minnetonka in that Prince movie, and I just have to laugh. I think of that Dave Chappelle skit, the one where he dresses up like Prince. And he tells Charlie Murphy to go purify himself in the waters of Lake Minnetonka. I love that episode. And that's what I'm gonna do. I'm gonna get in this Mercedes and purify my whole self by driving around and having a good day.

The leather inside is soft and colored like warm cream. And the car drives smoothly. So smoothly. I could steer with one finger if I wanted to. When I put in the infrared key, I feel like I am starting up a spaceship. Putting it in gear and driving down the road, I feel like one of the clouds came down from the gray sky and let me jump inside of it so I could ride it around.

I pick up one friend to ride around with. We hooped earlier. I can be a decent basketball player because I'm big. I know that. I get food with a friend later, and he says we need to go to Cup Foods on Chicago Avenue. I have been there before. Many times, actually. Ask anyone there. They know me. They know I love the world.

We make a bunch of other stops before we get to Cup Foods late in the evening around 7:30 p.m. My friend wants to buy a laptop from there. All the places in the world for laptops, but he wants one from there. Figures he will save money on it. He has been talking about their laptops all day. And that store, they sell everything. Cigarettes, chips, phones—everything. But I don't want much from there. We hang out for a bit because my friend says the computer doesn't work right. So he ends up in a long conversation about it. I can wait.

A couple of people I know come in. Someone says something funny. I laugh—I like to laugh. A big, mouth-wide-open, show-all-of-your-teeth-and-tonsils kind of laugh. Another friend of mine, a woman, comes in. She is always straight to the point, and she looks like she doesn't have time for any foolishness today. She's good people though. She gives good hugs. I think that I needed a good hug today.

While my friend is taking care of his laptop situation, I get some cigarettes. Maybe I want a banana too. Something to eat while I wait. I definitely want cigarettes. The young kid that sells them to me seems cool. I give him money and we chop it up for a bit. Then my friend gets his money back. I guess the laptop situation didn't work out right.

We head outside to the car. We chat a little bit. I joke about that cheap-ass laptop he almost got ripped off for. Then I get that infrared key ready to start the Mercedes. I start to feel funny—anxious, really—just before I can put the key in the ignition. Then I hear a loud tapping on my window.

"Look out your window," my friend says to me.

"Oh," I say, a bit startled. When I see who is there, even my hands jump from the steering wheel.

"Let's see your hands," I hear the officer say on the other side of the window. I get a sinking feeling in my stomach. I open the door. With the car not powered, it is the fastest way that I think of to give the officer access to whatever he may ask from me.

"Stay in the car!" he shouts.

"S-sorry," I stammer. I am anxious. Because I am big. And I am Black. I know that. I look like a fighter. But really, I am not that kind of guy.

"Let me see your other hand," the officer shouts again.

Then I am looking down the barrel of his gun.

"I'm sorry," I say again. "I didn't do nothing." I feel the need to say this because I am sorry. I didn't do anything. Except that I did: I am big. I know that. And I look like a threat. I am sorry. I am sorry that I looked like someone who needed to have a gun pointed at him.

"Show me your fucking hands, right now!"

My hands are up, but they must not be where he can see them. This does not occur to me. But that doesn't mean I am reaching for something. I am not. I am only sorry. And I am big. And I am Black. I know that.

"Put your hands up there!" the officer yells.

Where? In the air? They are already up there.

"Keep your fucking hands on the wheel," the officer commands.

My heart is racing now. My mouth is moving. I know that. I am not communicating to him like I want to. I know that too. Because he's still yelling at me. But if I can just tell him about my past experiences, maybe he will know that my heart is racing in my chest. I know he is scared too. I am sorry. But I am big. And I am Black. Let me explain.

"I got shot," I say, keeping both of my hands where he can see them.

"Keep your fucking hands on the wheel," the officer says again.

"Yes, sir," I say, complying. I never noticed how big my hands look on that Mercedes steering wheel. But they swallow it up.

"I'm sorry, Officer," I try to explain again. "But I got shot before—"

"Who else is in the car?" the officer interrupts.

"That's my friend," I say. Beside me, I can see that my friend is explaining himself to the police officer too. I hope that it is going well. I think to communicate my anxiety once more to the officer.

"I got shot the same way—before," I explain. His voice is still raised. So is his gun.

"Okay, but when I say let me see your hands, you put your fucking hands up."

"Okay, I'm sorry, Mr. Officer." My heart pounds in my chest.

"Get out of the car," the officer demands.

"Okay," I say, but I do not move. "Please, don't shoot me."

"I need you to step out of the car and step away from me," the officer orders.

I am relieved he puts his gun away, but still I cannot move from the car. Taking me by the wrist, the officer pulls me from the car, and I let him. Because I can move a whole lot. And it takes a whole lot to move me. I know that. And I'm no angel. I know that too. I have done things I am not proud of. I have served time in prison. I have had the police at my door for stupid things I have done. And I have had them at my door for more sinister things. I know that. But that was a long time ago. And a man can change. I believe that. I want to make a living for my kids. But I lost one job after an accident and then lost the other because of COVID-19. The officer knows that. He used to work that job too.

A different officer takes over once they have me in handcuffs. He walks me across the street and sits me on the ground.

"All right, what's your name?" he asks as he pulls a pen and pad from his belt.

"George," I say. My voice is panicked. My heart is racing. I whimper. But I can't help that my voice is coming out the way it is.

"Do you know why we're here?" the officer asks.

"Why?"

"Because it sounds like you gave a fake bill to the individuals in there. Are you on something right now?"

"No," I say. But I am. They know that. And my heart is racing. And the world is closing in all around me. When they open the door to the squad car, it looks like they are opening a casket for me to lie in.

"I'm claustrophobic," I say as they push six feet and four inches and one-hundred eighty pounds of panic into the back seat.

"Take a seat," the officer commands.

"I'm going in," I reply.

"No, you're not!" he says, raising his voice. He is right. I was not sitting down. And he sounds as panicked as I feel. I try again to communicate my angst. I am big. I am Black. I have done some bad things. I know that.

"I'm not that kind of guy," I say nevertheless. Because I am not. I am not the man who sits in the back of police cars. I am trying to be better. I want to be better. I want to have a message for young Black men coming after my generation because they are lost. "I'm not that kind of guy," I say again because I don't want to be. Because getting in the back of another police squad car is so many steps back from the steady progress I've made over nearly a decade. And when they try to place me in that coffin, I claw my way back out as fast as I can. They don't see the struggle I make to be a better man. I have to prove it to them somehow.

"I'll die!" I wail as they continue to crush my frame into that seat. My heart pounds and my chest tightens.

"Stop fighting!" an old man says on the sidewalk. Somehow, his voice is louder to me than the officers' voices. "You can't win!" the old man shouts. He doesn't know about my fight either. When they finally succeed in getting me in the back seat, I push through to the other side. Death doesn't have me yet. But it's close. I can feel it.

Soon, I feel like an enormous weight is on my chest. My breaths come, but I cannot breathe deeply. At first, I think they are holding down my chest, but they are behind me.

"Just let me kneel," I say. Because if I can just kneel, I can at least get some air into my lungs. But they aren't listening. They are forcing me down. Down. Down to the ground. I can move a whole lot. And it takes a whole lot to move me. I know that. It takes three of them to keep me on the ground. One of them keeps my legs still. A second holds my torso. And a third, my former coworker, puts his knee on my neck. Why should my neck be restrained at all? It can't go anywhere without my body. I know because the life is slowly fading from my body. And it seems very much that my head will go with it.

"I can't breathe," I say. Because I can't. Not like I want to. Not deep and full like a man singing about freedom. No, my breaths are shallow in my chest. That my chest is stamped against the ground does not help. Nor does it help my throat to be knelt upon when I am simply trying to explain something to the police officers. All I have been trying to explain to them is all that I cannot find words for.

I am big. I am Black. I know that. And I'm sorry that scares you. It scares me too. Because I am not that kind of guy. My chest is big and powerful. But even it can struggle to hold my heart still when the world proves too much for it. Even it can struggle to fill with air when it is being held down.

With my last breaths, I call for my mother even though I know she cannot hear me. I cry out for her even though I know she won't wipe my tears. I tell my people how much I love them. I am grateful for what I can say. And I try to make one last appeal.

"Just let me stand," I say. But they won't hear me.

I am big. I am Black. I am gone.

The police officers kneeled over me. They were frantic as they attempted to administer CPR. But they were far too late. They did not stop to think about my life until long after it was possible to revive me. I wished they had cared just moments before.

* * *

When I finally recognized Melody's face in front of me, she was no longer smiling. Perhaps her expression was mirroring mine. Watching the George Floyd case unfold on the news and on social media felt to me like Botham's murder was happening all over again. Yes, the cases had their differences, but there were enough similarities. The CPR that came far too late was the one that hurt me most. It was, for me, the indication that they had forgotten to protect and serve. Melody took note of the pain in my eyes. Then she held up three fingers, and the session continued.

* * *

I save lives. That is what I do. Every day, I am the woman with you when the unimaginable has happened. And we can imagine so many things. Almost everything in life can be imagined, even things we have not lived yet. We can imagine being in love, what the person looks like, how that person will treat us. But we cannot imagine things not in life. We cannot imagine death. Not really. We can imagine dying. But we cannot fully fathom the idea that we won't be here anymore. And when tragedy strikes, when we are face-to-face with that very notion, I am here. To keep you from leaving here. If I can.

I have been on the front lines of the pandemic from the beginning, and I am exhausted. I just want to curl up with my man and a movie and get as much sleep as I can. We had our first confirmed cases last week, and we may even shut down soon. The coming days are only going to get crazier.

On my way home, I get a call from Kenneth.

"You want me to bring anything home?" he asks. "Food or something?"

He always checks on me. And don't I deserve that? I spend all day checking on other people. It's nice when people check on me for a change.

I have the house to myself when I get home. There is a bedroom for my sister, but she won't be home tonight. Just me and bae. And something lighthearted. I don't need any more drama in my movies. I don't need any more drama in my love life either. I'm not gonna bad-mouth anyone. My ex went about his life the best way he knew how. I'm not gonna sit here and judge him for the way he lived. I'll leave that to God. But his lifestyle wasn't for me. And his love don't live here anymore.

Kenneth has been good to me. We've been off again and on again for seven years. We have been through a lot together. I know he loves me. And we have our ups and downs. But he is not full of drama like my ex was. And I don't need drama. Not in my house. Not in my movies. I got enough of it at work.

Tonight is a low-key night. It is already cool and breezy when I get home. The clouds are bright against the black sky, and a light drizzle patters across the parking lot to my apartment. A few leaves, old and brown, remain from last autumn. They stick to the pavement and the mat in front of my door. My mat says "Welcome." The one in front of my neighbor's says "Nothing inside is worth dying for." It makes me laugh sometimes. I guess that is one way to keep the drama away.

I don't remember when I fell asleep during the movie. I don't even remember falling asleep. But I remember waking up. The knock at the door was like thunder. My boyfriend is already out of bed, a gun in his hand. Again, thunder sounds from down the hall.

"Who is at the door at this time?" Kenneth asks incredulously. I get out of bed and follow him to the door. We hear the knock again. Loud and terrifying. No one knocks at the door like that at an hour like this unless they mean to harm someone.

"Who's there?" I shout down the dark hallway. There are no lights on, and looking at the path to the door is like having my eyes closed. But that darkness seems to swell with the heaviness of the knocks at the door.

"Who's there?" I yell again. There is another knock. Then there is a sound louder than thunder. Someone means to knock my door down. I think to go back into the bedroom, but before I can move, the door explodes off the hinges. It is still dark, but the man at the threshold is darker.

Boom!

There is a flash of light beside me, and I feel Kenneth grab my hand. But it is too late. I cannot move. It seems that lights flash everywhere around me, and the sounds that ring throughout the house are deafening. Glass shatters in my living room. Cabinets in my kitchen slam open. Walls splinter all around me. But I cannot move.

Somewhere, a woman screams. The screams are both far from and near to me at the same time.

I save lives. That's what I do. I am the woman with you when the unimaginable happens. Can you imagine what it is like to be dying? And your last thought is that you will never know why you died?

* * *

"That is how Botham died," I said to Melody. "His death was completely incomprehensible to him. His killer sat in that court and said to my face that being in a room with someone you shot is the scariest thing anyone can imagine. She never imagined what it was like to face a cop when you have committed no criminal act.

"That's what Arbery felt when he was being chased. That is what Breonna felt when she was awakened to gunfire. It is what my brother felt. One moment he was eating ice cream; the next moment he was trying to explain to a cop why she shouldn't kill him while also wondering why a cop would want to kill him. I will carry that thought in my head every day for the rest of my life.

"And every time a new act of police brutality happens, I relive that phone call I got on the day Botham was killed. How am I supposed to ever get over that?"

Melody looked at me with a sympathetic expression.

"I don't know," she said with her calm and soothing voice. And she still held up two fingers. And she still moved them back and forth.

* * *

I protect mine. I am truly not a violent woman. But I will do what I need to do to protect me and mine. And I have a right to do that. As a Black woman, I am justified in doing it. As an American, I am entitled by the Constitution. You know, that piece of paper that names and protects human rights in this country? Yes, I know what it does because I am not a violent woman. But I am an educated one. I just graduated pre-med from Xavier University, and one day I will use my education to save lives. But that's for the future. Today, I am watching my nephew and supporting his video game habit.

"Boy, do you know what time it is?" I ask after entering the living room and watching over his shoulder for a few minutes.

"Just a little longer," he replies. It is a captivating game, I suppose. But it is almost three o'clock in the morning. I think to lecture him about the importance of sleep for an eight-year-old boy, but I decide that he isn't hurting anyone. After all, it is Saturday.

"Well, I am going to bed," I say. I turn to head to my bedroom, but I hear a sound outside the house. Three in the morning is a terrible time to hear noises outside of your house. Especially so close to the window. I look at my nephew, and it is clear that he has heard what I heard.

"Stay here," I say, trying my best not to alarm him. "I'll be right back."

I head to my room where I store a handgun and return to the living room, gun in hand. The blinds are drawn on the window. I hear another noise in that area and begin to approach slowly. I make sure I have a round chambered. Then I get right up to the window and pull the blinds open.

"Put your hands up!" a man yells at the closed window. "Show me your hands!"

That's it.

That's the last thing I heard.

* * *

"That was the news that awaited me a few days after I got back from Botham's trial," I explained to Melody. "Do you understand? Lots of people are outraged from behind their televisions and their smartphones. It never stops for me."

Melody put her index finger down and sighed almost imperceptibly. I am sympathetic to her efforts, but I also think that enough people are *desensitized* to police brutality. I am not sure I want to stop feeling this pain. I may need to feel this pain. It's the injustice that needs to stop.

Chapter Twenty-Two

I could only see Botham in my dreams, so I wanted to stay there. I didn't want to stop feeling the pain, and maybe that's why depression followed me. Melody once asked me if I had any unfinished business with Botham. I gave her an answer that expressed some pain, but the truth was even more painful. There was so much that I still wanted to say to Botham. And I could only do that in my dreams.

"Hello, sis," he said, grinning so broadly and contagiously that I had to laugh. "You'll never guess why they're sending us home."

"Why's that?" I asked.

"Rain!" he said, chuckling. "Can you believe that?"

"That sounds ridiculous," I said. "Did you get my text message?"

"The one about the dude who burned down his house?" Botham said, laughing louder.

"Yes!" I said. "How crazy is that? Imagine hating Kaepernick so much that you not only burn your Nikes, but you accidentally burn down the house too!"

"That is a special level of hate," Botham said. "I can't imagine hating anyone or anything that much."

"Well," I said, "welcome to America."

"Hey," he challenged me, "you came here first."

"And I don't regret it . . . most of the time." I sat in traffic that only crept forward every minute or so. Traffic was not my favorite thing about the United States. Though I felt like a New Yorker—I had been here almost twenty years now—even though Saint Lucia would always be home, I preferred the hustle and bustle of New York to the ambling lifestyle of my childhood.

"Do you think we can convince Brandt to come to the states?" I asked.

"I've been working on it," Botham replied. "Honestly, I don't know what he would want to do out here. Sometimes, I think I left him in Saint Lucia too soon. He was always a bit sensitive."

"And you have his ear like nobody else," I remarked. "He looks up to you."

"Then I hope I am giving him a proper model to look up to."

"I know you are," I said.

"Only because you give good advice," Botham said. "If it weren't for your suggestions, I think he would have spent the entire time playing video games when he visited me here."

"But you figured it out," I said.

The traffic was beginning to lighten up, but I wished we would stay in gridlock forever. I didn't want this call with Botham to end. So I got out of the fast lane and into the middle lane where the traffic was much slower.

"Do you know that he prays for you every day?" I asked.

"Of course he does," Botham replied. "And I pray for him. We all pray for each other, I hope."

"Yes, but he does a special prayer for you," I said. "I do too. You know Black men need all the prayer they can get here."

"I know," he replied. "Me and Brandt talk about it all the time, about how to be around police officers. Don't argue with them; be respectful; pay attention to who you hang around, where you are, and at what time. The worst place for a Black man to be is in the wrong place at the wrong time. But Brandt is a good boy; he'll listen."

"And what about you?" I asked. "If a police officer pulls you over for being Black, what will you do?"

"Oh, I'm the charming one," Botham said with a smile. "We'll be best friends by the time the conversation is over."

"Yeah, a best friend can still give you a traffic ticket," I said mockingly.

"And if I get away with just a traffic ticket," he rebutted, "I will consider myself a very lucky man."

"Hopefully, that is never a path we'll have to cross," I said. There was a quiver in my voice as the traffic quickened.

"What's wrong?" he asked.

"Oh, nothing," I stammered, preferring to keep the conversation lighthearted. What I wanted to do was warn him, to tell him that after this phone call, when he gets home, he will have to be sure that the door is closed—latched closed. And locked. But I knew I could not say anything; telling him would ruin the dream. And he would fade from my dreams, where I was hoping to keep him forever.

"What's wrong, sis?" he asked. "You look like you want to tell me something."

"Oh, no," I replied. A solitary tear rolled down my face. "It's just that there are so many police shootings every year. I guess I just worry about you sometimes."

"Are there really that many?" he asked.

"Don't do that," I replied. "Don't talk like them, like the ones who throw out statistics as if the number of Black men who kill other Black men cancel out the number of police officers who do it. Don't be like them, the ones who deny police brutality is a thing because they've never had a police officer talk down to them as if they were not an adult. Don't . . ." I trailed off.

He threw back his head and let out an uproarious laugh. "I know, sis, I know. Gosh, it is so easy to get under your skin."

To this joyous response, I could not stop myself from letting out a sob. "Don't you know this has always been my worst nightmare? That I would lose you this way?"

"But you haven't lost me." His voice became soft and soothing.

"You were always too kind, too unsuspecting," I said.

"Unsuspecting?" Botham said, his voice musical with laughter. "Do you know where I am going to celebrate finally being pain-free after those dentists literally pulled bones from my skull? Do you know where I'll be? Home! I'm going to get my ice cream, and I am going to go straight home where it's safe."

"But you won't lock the door," I said with a quiet, self-reflective voice.

"Lock the door?" he said.

Again, I wished I could warn him.

You won't have to be outside your home for them to get you.

You won't have to be in the wrong place at the wrong time.

You won't have a gun on you.

You won't be on drugs.

You won't have a chance to be belligerent or combative.

You won't get a chance to resist arrest

They're still going to get you.

"Never mind," I said. As I got closer to my house, I knew the conversation was coming to an end. "Do you know, you forgot to tell me last time we spoke?" I asked.

"Tell you what?"

"That you love me," I replied. "You should say it now before—"

But it was too late. My eyes opened, and I was staring at the ceiling in my bedroom.

The next time I dreamed of Botham, he was in my kitchen, cooking a meal. I wished again that I could tell him something about his fate, but I had to keep him here.

I lived in a house in Brooklyn when Botham was alive, but after my divorce was finalized, my sons and I moved to Queens. But the house in Brooklyn was still new in my dreams. The kitchen was still shiny with its brown oak cabinets, shiny black marble countertops, and black appliances. Of course, Botham made an absolute mess of those countertops. It seemed that every herb I owned and half the contents of my refrigerator were beside the stove, waiting to be added to the cream sauce. I loved to watch him cook—even if he did dice vegetables with a steak knife. I had an entire block of knives for cooking, but he was determined to use that little steak knife to cut everything.

"You know, there are better knives," I said to him. But he only grinned and continued cutting.

"When you taste this food," he said, "you aren't going to care about the knife I used."

As we sat down to eat, it became obvious to Botham that something was wrong. "Where is everybody?" he asked. "I made enough for the whole family."

We both looked around at the emptiness in the house, and a funny feeling sank into the pit of my stomach. He does not know how things have been made different since he passed. My husband is now my ex. Botham's nephews are big, so much bigger now. Jaydan is almost his uncle's height. And Botham could not be allowed to see any of them. I no longer dream of my ex-husband, and if Botham knew how his nephews had changed, he would disappear, and I would be forced to wake up. So I filled the silence and tried to keep Botham's attention away from the darkness that encroached on us from all corners of the house.

"You taught Brandt a new song?" I said, hoping to change the subject.

"I did," he replied. "How did you know?"

"He sang it at—" I had almost made a fatal error when a heavy knock shook the front door. Grateful for an excuse to escape the conversation, I stood hastily and approached the door. As I stood there, it occurred to me that I had no idea who could be at the door. I hesitated, and the heavy knock sounded once more.

Boom! Boom!

I stood frozen before the door. As I was thinking that I shouldn't open it, it flew open and a White woman in a police uniform stood in the threshold with her gun drawn.

"Botham!" I cried as he appeared from the kitchen. I heard a gunshot ring out, but Botham remained unscathed. I looked down then to see that the bullet had pierced my own chest. As I fell to the ground, Botham rushed to my side, getting to me just in time for me to fall into his arms.

"You have to wake up, Allisa," he said solemnly.

"I can't," I replied.

"You're going to die in here if you don't wake up."

"No," I said. "I will die if I do."

"You won't," he said. "You still have much to do."

"Like what?" I asked.

"Well, you still have to look out for me," he replied, "just as you always have. That task may look a little different, but I still need you to be my big sis."

"How can I do that when there are parasites trying to live off your name?"

"You can do it because you aren't concerned with them. You're concerned with me and others like me. You honor my memory by fighting for the living, not dwelling on the dead. Those who would exploit tragedy are dead. You staying in this bed is you waiting to die. But you must live!"

In the far distance, I could hear what sounded like an ambulance's siren.

"They're coming for me," I said.

"That's not for you," Botham said.

"Then who is it for?"

"You'll see when you get up."

I looked over to the doorway and saw several police officers. Some were plain-clothed, some were in uniform, and others wore full tactical gear. My heart still ached, but when I looked down, I did not see a hole in my chest. Instead, it was quite the opposite: my heart was so full it was heavy. And yet Botham lifted me with so little effort.

I rose from the floor and moved toward the door with a strength I had never known I could have. When I looked back, the entire apartment was cloaked in darkness. Botham was no longer back there, but I felt he was with me all the same. When I returned my gaze to the open door before me, every police officer knelt.

I walked forward, across the threshold, to see that each of them held their own handcuffs. They made a path for me and shackled their own wrists as I walked by them. Then they faded into the darkness behind me as I walked toward a light that became brighter and brighter with every step.

Chapter Twenty-Three

I lay wide awake in the bed. It seemed that I was coming out of a fever. My pillow, sheets, and blankets were drenched in sweat. I had a clarity of thought akin to the feeling one gets when the sinuses finally clear themselves of the virus that had seized them with restricted breathing and arrested sleep. I sat up and grabbed my phone where I noted several missed calls and messages.

I'll deal with those later, I thought. It was approaching the one-year anniversary of the Botham Jean Act being passed. It stipulated that police officers were not allowed to turn off their body cameras when they were actively participating in an investigation. The Texas governor passed it, and it was set to go into effect near the anniversary of Botham's death. I needed to look at it today. I needed to know that some ground was being made in this struggle for justice. But as I searched the internet, I instead came across news that Amir Locke's killers would not stand trial.

Not again, I thought, my despair threatening to keep me shackled in my bed. I took a deep breath in anticipation of the wave of darkness to come.

However, it did not come. Instead, I felt compelled to jump out of my bed and begin pacing my bedroom floor. And so, I did just that. I read the news article once. Then a second and a third time. My first thought was that I needed to get in touch with his family.

This can't keep happening. They can't keep getting away with this.

My next thought was about the fever dream I'd had last night where rows of police officers knelt in handcuffs. Those who were guilty. Those who killed with extreme malice. Those who were negligent in their duties. Those who tried to help others cover up their crimes. They had to be brought to justice. And any unjust laws they served needed to be eradicated. The police officers who killed Amir belonged in that group. As my anger welled up inside me, I surprised myself by opening the video application on my phone and searching for clips depicting Amir's death. When I found one, I did not hesitate to open it.

"Police, stay clear!" they had shouted, one officer's voice over the other's so that there was no way Amir could have understood them if he were awake. But he was not awake. So silently, so gently did they slide that key into the apartment door before they charged into the room with enough flashing lights to give a person an epileptic seizure and so much sudden noise that Amir might have died of a heart attack. If the bullet had not gotten to him first. He had no last words. He probably did not even know what was happening.

Like Bo . . .

I watched the video several more times, my heart breaking just a little more each time. Botham also did not have time to know what was happening. And there was no body-cam footage. I watched Amir's footage over and over, and I wondered if that was how quickly Guyger had killed Botham.

Part of the torture I endured, living with the guilt that I could not be near Botham when he needed me most, also included the fact that I could only *imagine* what had happened that night. I would never truly know. Botham could not tell me. All I had to go on was Guyger's testimony—the one she'd given with the hope she would elude justice.

I wanted to know the truth of what happened so badly that I'd even written Amber a letter once. I could not say that it was a kind letter. I did not even address her by name. I could not bring myself to write her name. Besides that, how would I address her?

Dear . . .

Ma'am . . .

Greetings . . .

Hello, I hope this letter finds you well . . .

None of those words fit. I remembered dating the letter. Maybe there was an address. I couldn't even remember exactly what I wrote. It was probably curt.

Tell me what he said! You owe me that much.

She did not reply to it. She replied to some of the members at my church. I knew that much. And Brandt. One time, I think she even asked how I was doing. But she referred to me as Brandt's sister. Definitely not by my name. That my church had reached out to Amber Guyger and that they had a back-and-forth correspondence incensed me; my own church was checking on my brother's killer, but I never got the sense they ever felt obligated to check on me.

Definitely not Botham's sister.

In the place of her response, I listened to her 911 emergency call. Too many times. It probably was not healthy for me to listen to it once. I listened to it more than once.

"I'm inside the apartment with him," she had said. I would lean in closer to my speakers every time I got to the part where she said that. I always thought that I could hear Botham groaning in the background.

"Hey! Come on, man," she had said.

Right there. Just before, and maybe right after.

But that was all I had.

I found a little solace when Texas passed Bo's Law. It would not bring Botham back. It might not have even prevented his murder. But it would have shed light on the matter. It would have given us a view of Guyger's mental state and actions as she entered Bo's apartment. It had certainly shed light on the kind of officers Breonna Taylor dealt with.

"Keep walking backward!" one of those officers had shouted at Kenneth, her boyfriend, after she had been killed.

"Walk back to me or I'll send this dog!" the officer shouted while the dog barked ferociously and Kenneth cried and wondered helplessly why Breonna had been killed.

"I'm scared," he whimpered.

"Oh, you're scared?" the man scoffed.

Because Black men can't be scared. They are only scary. They need to be yelled at, beaten down, torn apart by dogs, and shot if necessary. They can be scary. But they can't be scared.

"What's going on?" Kenneth asked.

"You're going to f—king prison. That's what's going on," the officer answered.

What a charming sense of humor.

As they led him away in cuffs, he lamented, "My girlfriend is dead."

"I don't give a—" the woman police officer began but stopped herself. "Keep walking!" she screamed instead.

She must have remembered that her body cam was still on.

That female officer thought twice about what she was going to say. Maybe some officers would think twice about what they would do if they knew they were always being monitored. Maybe Guyger would have paid better attention to her surroundings if she knew she was not the only one paying attention to them. Or maybe not. She tried to hide behind the Castle Doctrine even though it was not her house. She was not the first officer to try hiding behind the law in order to get away with murder, and she would not be the last.

Amir Locke's killers wore body cams. But they were going to take care of a military threat. Amir was just a casualty of that battle. No need to send anyone to jail over collateral damage. Breonna Taylor faced the same circumstance, casualty of war. They killed her with their first shots. The only thing that might have been different if those detectives were wearing body cameras is that no shots would have been fired into the living room. Or the bedroom, where Breonna's sister could have been made collateral damage as well. So I knew I would keep trying to get the law changed for qualified immunity. I was encouraged by Bo's Law if for no other reason than from the moment of its passing, Botham's name would forever be in the law books, in the police training, and on the lips of every police officer, lawyer, and politician.

For the same reason that I celebrated Bo's Law, I felt encouraged by the unanimous vote that turned a portion of Lamar Street, the most important portion where the Dallas Police Department and the scene of Guyger's crime resided, into Botham Jean Boulevard. I took some solace in it despite there being more work to be done—and in spite of the minor troubles it brought me. As I thought about those troubles, I picked up my phone and returned to the text messages I had noted upon waking. I had made a simple request:

"Can you remove Queen?" I had asked Adam in reference to a social media page for the Botham Jean Memorial Commission that still included her photo on its banner.

"Of course," he had replied. Queen was still fuming over the $84,000 she had missed out on in her attempt to profit from renaming the street. A close inspection of her social media showed that she had made a living and an entire persona off the tragedies of police brutality. She had been keen to do the same to Botham until she realized that I would not let her do it at my expense. Then she blocked me on all her social media. So I see no reason her photo should be on a webpage dedicated to Botham. Adam did not agree, but he wanted to stay in my good graces, I suppose, so he honored my request. Halfway.

When I looked up the webpage after seeing his text, I saw that her face was still in the profile picture. I picked up my phone and sent Adam another text.

"She is still there."

"Where?"

"In the profile picture."

"Oh, sorry."

I continued to look through the website and found a few more things that disturbed me. There was a link to an article about the street renaming. I picked up the phone and called him.

"Adam," I said when he picked up.

"Hey, queen!" he said with feigned surprise.

"You can call me Allisa," I replied shortly. "Look, I just read an article that states that you feel your efforts to rename that street were appropriated?"

"Oh," he replied. "Let me look into that."

"It's on your webpage," I said, trying to remain calm. "And you did a shout-out of the article on social media."

"I did?"

"You know you did."

"Uhh . . ."

"So you and your council members think getting the name changed was *bittersweet*?" I asked.

"Well, yes," he said. "Do you know what I went through to get those petitions?"

"And they paid off," I said. "They renamed the street."

"Yeah!" he replied with a high-pitched squeal. "But we were kind of left out of the loop."

"Yes. You were left out of the eighty-four thousand dollar loop. But aren't you glad that it didn't cost that much?" I knew that he was not.

"Sure," he said. "But that didn't exactly help us out."

"I was not aware that you needed help," I said. "I thought this was about Botham."

"It is," he said. "But we all gotta eat, right?"

"Is that why you're in this? To eat? You know I have a full-time job for that, right?"

He was silent. I let him simmer in that silence for a while before he gave in. "Look, what do you want me to do?"

"Rename your committee," I said. "It is clear that you are not in this for Botham."

"Of course we are," he said almost pleadingly. "Look, what if I delete the link from the website."

"Yes. Do that. And don't post anything else about Botham. You got what you were looking for; they renamed the street."

"There are still more things we can do for you," he said, trying to convince me. "I mean, why not get the whole street renamed?"

"Let me worry about that."

"Look, it's segregated!" he said in a final effort to convince me. "It's like they have a whole Jim Crow street going on in Dallas. We can get that whole street renamed. We will put people on the ground over there. Move the masses. We'll get petitions signed. We'll—"

"Charge somebody else tens of thousands of dollars? Because it won't be me."

"Listen—"

"Don't post anything else on the website."

"But—"

"That's all." I hung up, wondering how long it would be before he blocked me on social media too.

I sighed deeply and looked at the time. I had an appointment with Melody. I could not wait to tell her what I'd learned today.

Chapter Twenty-Four

One year.

That is how long I have been seeing Melody to help me with my post-traumatic stress. I avoided any kind of treatment for three years. And post-traumatic stress is exactly what I had. I was surprised to even learn I could have the condition.

I was not there when Botham was killed. Nevertheless, the murder shook me to my core. I replayed the shooting in my head before I knew what had happened. Then I replayed the shooting when I learned more details. When shootings continued to happen to Black people over the years, I then replayed those shootings. For three years, I experienced new shootings as if I were getting that phone call again. I became shell-shocked to every new murder, every news report.

Shell-shocked.

Like I had gone to war. Because it is as though the police are at war with us. Watching them conduct no-knock warrants is like watching the military conduct a raid on a hostile nation. And still, in the wake of my brother's death, I had to listen to citizens and politicians alike act as though they could not fathom a government at war with its citizens.

I, on the other hand, could not imagine how anyone would see the way Guyger had killed my brother and not think something was wrong with the system. Amber Guyger was given great power. And David Washington seemed to think that she should not be held responsible for the tragedy she caused with that power. Power without responsibility, that is what qualified immunity is. The United States should be a free country, for the people by the people. But we have qualified immunity on our books. And Black people have been relegated to casualties of war.

George Floyd? Casualty of war. He used a counterfeit bill and was trying to overcome a drug addiction, so now his life is not worth worrying about. Let him die under your knee!

Eric Garner? He might have been selling loose cigarettes without the state's approval. Get over there and kill him!

Breonna Taylor? She once dated a drug dealer. He may or may not be in her house. Go in there and kill her!

Atatiana Jefferson? Her front door is open past midnight. Peek in her window and kill her!

Amir Locke? His cousin allegedly killed someone. Go in that cousin's house and kill anyone who wakes up the wrong way!

Botham Jean? He was at home. Go in there and kill him!

People watched these killings on television but could not fathom a government at war with its citizens. But the US government has been at war with Black Americans since the Emancipation Proclamation was signed. They could no longer enslave us, so the Black Codes came. Then Jim Crow. Then the War on Drugs. One after the other after the other. At no point in US history have the police not been in a position to treat Black neighborhoods like war zones and keep Black citizens in its crosshairs. Botham had been in the United States for six short years before a police officer—who was once so bored and peeved to be doing her *primary* job at an MLK parade—ran into his apartment like special forces and put Botham in her crosshairs. She treated Botham like a military threat. So, yeah. Post-traumatic stress. That's just one of the conditions I had to be treated for.

Three years.

That's how long it took me to stop shaking. Or at least shake less frequently. Melody tried everything with me. My eyes followed her index finger with the hope it would lead my mind out of its labyrinth of trauma. The last time she tried this EMDR treatment, my eyes played no tricks on me. I saw only the one finger. And I only had one incident to recall. I could not say that the incident was not traumatic. It was. What was different was my response to it. Rather than feeling helpless and sorry, I felt a powerful indignation.

I am not your agenda. I am a human being. I did not choose to be born, nor did I choose where I would be born and raised. All I can say is that I am trying to get to a better place. I know that it is easy to make a judgment of me from afar. I am Black and I stay strapped.

If I were White, I'd be considered as American as apple pie, just a US citizen exercising my Second Amendment right to keep those who would do me harm from carrying out their worst wishes on me. Self-defense, right? I need it. I sleep with it. Because I want to keep waking up and deal with the hand I have been dealt. Until I can get my hands on different cards. Or join another game altogether. I do have dreams. And every night I go to sleep. And I exercise my constitutional right to ensure that I wake up and stay up.

"He woke up to become a casualty of war," I said to Melody, who finally brought her hands to rest in her lap. "Right?"

"I don't follow," she replied.

"What is the justification for his death?" I asked. "That he was in the wrong place at the wrong time? Do the police have a blank check to kill anyone inside of a home that has been served a no-knock warrant? Whoever is on the other side of that door has no right to life because the people serving these warrants go in there to kill."

"But it seems like you feel a little different about this case than previous ones," Melody noted.

"Do I?" I asked.

"Yes," she said. "And this one is not exactly like your brother's death. Botham was not armed."

"They are all like my brother in that they were all innocent. Period. In which of these situations can you point to the victim and say, 'This person was committing a crime'? Certainly not Botham's.

But what was Breonna doing? Ahmaud? Amir? Imagine being someone who could excuse these victims' deaths by anything they were doing when they encountered the police."

"Mhmm." Melody nodded, though she did not seem to be responding to what I was saying. "So it seems you have found your voice."

"I don't know about that." I said, "But I think I am getting a clearer idea of what I am supposed to do."

"And what do you think that is?" Melody asked.

"I am supposed to keep fighting," I replied.

"For Botham?"

"For me."

This was another condition Melody was treating me for. Somehow, in my grief for Botham, I had started losing my own identity. Everything I did was for Botham. I wore red for Botham. I chased politicians around the country, trying to get them to change laws. For Botham. I still can't celebrate most holidays because I can't do them for Botham.

Throughout the past year of treatment, when I mentioned some goal that I wanted to accomplish or some activity I wanted to avoid, I had to ask myself if my actions were for me or for Botham. I discovered that so many of my actions had become an act of grieving. I had to learn actions that helped me heal. I suppose there was and always will be a thin line between grieving and healing. I was learning to tell the difference.

As I drove home from that day's session, I took the moment to be present and appreciate being present. Even cloudy days in New York can be beautiful.

My drive reveals a winding highway lined with budding and flowering trees. Passing Central Park, I admire the maple-lined reservoir and the buildings that stretch so high in the backdrop. But more than these, I enjoy the feel of the car that I command across these roads and down these highways. I stop at red lights and make turns, fully aware of my destination.

I drive in silence. At times, I simply listen to the sound of the engine, but mostly I think about the things that need to be done to get justice for Amir Locke. I had spoken with his mother earlier that week, after the Minnesotan courts decided not to pursue charges against the police officers who killed him.

"It's just a reminder of how much work there is still left to do," I told her.

"But how can they not see that his death was wrong?" she cried.

"Because they don't see their laws as unjust," I replied. "But we'll be changing that."

"And in the meantime?" she asked. "How am I supposed to take that? My son lost his life, and I am supposed to just accept that as a fact of life?"

"No," I said.

"Am I supposed to even seek some kind of closure on this?"

"There is no closure," I said. "Not in the traditional sense. Our closure will always be fleeting, so we will have to always seek it out. Our closure is in the fight. We must never stop fighting. It's a tough road to navigate, but I have unearthed some of the path forward, and I will share it with you."

I found a certain strength in my ability to tell her this. Because I did know the path forward. I had been on it for the past four years, and I could reach back and provide a guiding hand. Furthermore, I knew what she was going through. Amir was not a criminal, and he was not an agenda. He was a human being. He wanted to move to Dallas. He wanted to be a musician. He had friends and family who were charmed by his humor; who wanted to see what kind of man he would become; who smiled when he entered a room. He had done nothing wrong, but he lost his life. And those who loved him had their love replaced by grief.

I understood this because I had loved and lost. That is what those on the outside looking in seem to forget. Victims of police brutality are not there to give you purpose—not as a lawmaker, not as a law enforcer, and not as an activist.

The people who want to create and uphold laws forget that laws are meant to protect the freedom of real-life people first. The no-knock law goes after everyone who could ever be in the same house with a known target. And as we saw with Breonna and Amir, it goes after those innocent people while they are asleep. The law enforcement officers who killed Breonna and Amir were so concerned with getting their target, they forgot to even care about the people who had committed no crime, people who were not guilty by association, no matter how much character assassination the officers committed to try to justify their deaths afterward.

And just as there are lawmakers and enforcers who will sacrifice the freedom of citizens to the power they gain by punishing lawbreakers, there are activists who will sacrifice their pursuit of justice to their desire to gain moral clout from the victims of tragedy. You are not doing me a favor by protesting for Botham; you are denouncing an injustice. I owe you no favors for your act. Your payment for fighting against injustice is justice. If justice is not enough for you, go find something else to do.

Justice, or at the very least my continued fight for it, is what I could promise Amir and his family. I created the Botham Jean Foundation, and I cofounded Sisters of the Movement, a coalition of women from all races, and all of whom lost brothers to police brutality. I have watched these foundations grow strong so that I could provide a guiding and helping hand for families like Amir's. And now that I was doing the work to heal myself, I knew that I could also provide a steady hand. All of these thoughts not only filled the silence as I turned into my driveway, they also filled me with purpose as I parked in my garage and entered my home.

Inside, my boys are occupied with various tasks. Jordan is stretched out on the sofa with a video game in his hands. Jareem is on his way to his room upstairs with some food he has just heated up in the microwave. Jaydan walks around the living room chatting with a classmate about his upcoming graduation from high school.

It is a peculiar thing to look at your son all grown up, big and tall. As a mother, I will always see him as my baby, whom I had to carry to term, teach to walk and talk, and nurture into a man who is strong on the inside and the outside. It is a peculiar thing. I am both proud and afraid. He towers over me like Botham did, and he will only get bigger. I am proud to see him become a strong and kind man. I am afraid that people will see his strength before they ever know his kindness.

That is where I am five years after Botham's death. I am not quite where I want to be with God. I still pray with a bit of cynicism. I still look at some church members and feel that I have been betrayed. I still cry inconsolably when the congregation sings "You Are My Strength." And I have not forgiven Guyger for killing my brother. I do not know if I ever will. I am not sure if I can. I am not Brandt, and I have not even asked him what made him choose to forgive Guyger at the sentencing. But I stand by his right to make that choice. Maybe that is something he needed to do to heal, something he had to do for himself. I know what I will do for me. I will fight.

I want Botham's name to live on. I want people to know the kind of man he was. But most of all, I don't want to ever bury my son. No, my son will bury me as is the natural order of things. He will lay me to rest after I have fought long and hard to secure the kind of world he ought to live in.